THE World Cup 2018 Book

Shane Stay

THE World Cup
2018
Book

Everything you need to know about
the soccer World Cup

Meyer & Meyer Sport

British Library Cataloguing in Publication Data
A catalogue record for this book is available from the British Library

THE World Cup 2018 Book
Maidenhead: Meyer & Meyer Sport (UK) Ltd., 2018
ISBN: 978-1-78255-133-1

© 2018 by Meyer & Meyer Sport (UK) Ltd.
Aachen, Auckland, Berit, Cairo, Cape Town, Dubai, Hägendorf, Hong Kong, Indianapolis,
Manila, New Delhi, Singapore, Sydney, Tehran, Vienna

Credits
Design & Layout
Cover and Interior Design: Annika Naas
Layout: Amnet
Cover and Interior Photos: © picturealliance.com

Editorial
Managing Editor: Elizabeth Evans

Member of the World Sports Publishers' Association (WSPA), www.w-s-p-a.org
Printed by C-M Books, Ann Arbor, MI, USA
ISBN: 978-1-78255-133-1
Email: info@m-m-sports.com
www.m-m-sports.com

CONTENTS

INTRODUCTION

Every four years brings another World Cup, the people's game. It's the most anticipated sporting event in human history. Prior to Russia 2018, there were twenty crowned champions. It's an elite status, an honor.

It's also an honor to host the event. Russia was chosen by FIFA years in advance, not without a little controversy. Going backward in time, past hosts include Brazil, South Africa, Germany, Korea-Japan, France, United States, Italy, Mexico, Spain, Argentina, West Germany, Mexico, England, Chile, Sweden, Switzerland, Brazil, France, Italy, and Uruguay.

Following Russia, the next nation to host will be Qatar in 2022, not without a little more controversy. What's a World Cup without a little bit of drama? After all, it makes it more exciting.

For Russia, 2018 will be their first opportunity to host the World Cup. Leading up to the tournament, many new stadiums were erected, specially made for the World Cup. This is not uncommon; Brazil (2014) and South Africa (2010) did the same.

As it goes with each World Cup, those stadiums are filled with talented players from each of their respective countries, all hoping to get their hands on the illustrious Jules Rimet Trophy, as it used to be called. With track and field, you think Usain Bolt, Carl Lewis. With hockey, you think Wayne Gretzky, Mario Lemieux. With tennis, there are unforgettable names: Bjorn Bjorg, John McEnroe, Pete Sampras, Roger Federer. With American football, you have Joe Montana, Jerry Rice, Tom Brady, and many others. With soccer, World Cup champions make up an exclusive list, including: Pele, Garrincha, Maradona, Romario, Zidane, to name a few. But there are also the great teams, including Brazil 1970, Brazil 2002, Italy 2006, Spain 2010, and Germany 2014. Then, there are a few teams here and there that weren't champions, but made a big impact, including Brazil (1982) "arte de futbol," Cameroon (1990) "the indomitable lions," and South Korea (2002), the first Asian team to make the semifinals. Each World Cup creates the opportunity for new players to emerge, to stake a claim and join the fraternity of past winners. The most recent World Cup—Brazil 2014—carried on the great multimillion-dollar parade, a tradition that continues to this day.

Russia 2018 represents a legacy of dreams. For many countries, the ability to reach the World Cup is a major accomplishment. For others, they are expected to win every time.

With so many teams possessing the ability to win, the competition is great. It goes without saying, the winners achieve the status of number one in the world, and with that comes skill and a little luck. That's part of the beauty of the game. At some point in the tournament, even the best teams need a break here and there—whether that's the ball hitting off the post, an offside call that wasn't offside, a foul that wasn't called, or something else altogether, like Maradona's "Hand of God."

Uruguay kicked it off in 1930, and since then the winner's circle has been comprised of only a few nations.

To date, the winners are:

- Germany (2014)
- Spain (2010)
- Italy (2006)
- Brazil (2002)
- France (1998)
- Brazil (1994)
- West Germany (1990)
- Argentina (1986)
- Italy (1982)
- Argentina (1978)
- West Germany (1974)
- Brazil (1970)
- England (1966)
- Brazil (1962)
- Brazil (1958)
- West Germany (1954)
- Uruguay (1950)
- Italy (1938)
- Italy (1934)
- Uruguay (1930)

With billions of people watching, everyone is hoping that their team will join that elite list of champions. The excitement felt around the world is overwhelming. Beers will be flowing in the bars as the largest sporting event in history airs on TV.

The United States—which holds the record for highest attendance in World Cup history (World Cup 1994)—has bars across the nation which play host to passionate soccer fans from around the world. Fado Irish Pub in Atlanta, Philadelphia, Columbus, Chicago, and Seattle fills up with soccer fans excited for international games, and especially the World Cup.

The Atlantic Crossing—a popular soccer bar in Seattle, Washington—is ready to support World Cup 2018. Excitement for games at the bar reaches a fever pitch. Recalling World Cup 2014, Rissa (a manager) said US games were, "…packed, crazy." She added, "A front window was broken by accident, by fans pounding on the front window. It was literally so loud that we didn't hear the window break, but we saw it from behind the bar."

Although the US lost a crucial World Cup qualification game to Trinidad and Tobago on October 10, 2017, they should be back with a vengeance next time around.

Despite the US not making Russia 2018, bars like The Atlantic Crossing are filling up with eager fans around the country, who are reflecting on past World Cups to prepare for Russia in 2018.

A representative from Lou's City Bar in Washington, DC, recalled business from World Cup 2014, stating, "Sales went through the roof during the World Cup. The major domestics were on special, so Miller and Coors Light were very popular."

Looking forward to World Cup 2018, Dani, a manager from On Deck, a bar in Portland, Oregon, expects a variety of customers from different backgrounds. Referring to 2014, she said, "We got a lot of people from other countries. Very little English…either

French or Spanish was spoken [a lot]. The servers had trouble because they couldn't understand some of the people." Based on that experience, for World Cup 2018, she anticipates "a 25-40% increase in total sales."

Jay—who works at Goal, a popular bar in Los Angeles, California—expects a boost in sales from World Cup Russia. Many current and former professional players will stop by Goal for a visit. Jay said, "I anticipate it to be awesome."

In the Midwest, The Globe Pub in Chicago, Illinois, Amsterdam Tavern in St. Louis, Missouri, No Other Pub by Sporting KC in Kansas City, Missouri, and Fado Irish Pub in Columbus, Ohio, are bars that frequently cater to soccer audiences and should be off-the-wall crazy with World Cup action. Speaking as a representative of Fado Irish Pub in Columbus, Scott Neff said, "We are often chosen as one of the best soccer bars in the Midwest."

Around the world, bars from England, Germany, Japan, Egypt, Australia, Argentina, and Brazil—at every corner of the globe—will be filled to capacity with eager fans celebrating each game. People around the world would agree, soccer is simply the greatest.

Some of the rules and procedures for the World Cup have changed over the years. For instance, in 1994, there were 24 teams in the tournament. By 2018, FIFA allowed 32 teams to compete, representing all major soccer-playing nations. (We'll expound on these types of issues a bit later.) All 32 teams—from Europe, South America, North America, Africa to

Asia—went through a long qualification process* and have made history.

We'll look at each team, the players and coaches, and lay out each nuance of World Cup Russia.

Thanks for joining. Sit back and enjoy the ride. It only happens once every four years.

---

* Russia automatically qualified as the host nation.

FIFA World Cup
Original Trophy

FIFA World Cup
Original Trophy

CHAPTER 1

THE 32 TEAMS OF 2018
WORLD CUP RUSSIA

LIST OF TEAMS

EUROPE

Germany, Spain, England, France, Russia, Belgium, Croatia, Denmark, Iceland, Poland, Portugal, Serbia, Sweden, Switzerland

SOUTH AMERICA

Brazil, Argentina, Uruguay, Peru, Colombia

NORTH AMERICA

Costa Rica, Mexico, Panama

ASIA

Australia, Iran, Japan, Saudi Arabia, South Korea

AFRICA

Egypt, Morocco, Nigeria, Senegal, Tunisia

OCEANIA

(Oceania did not qualify a team this year.)

2018 WORLD CUP FINAL DRAW

Announced on December 1, 2017, in Moscow.

GROUP A

- Russia
- Saudi Arabia
- Egypt
- Uruguay

GROUP B

- Portugal
- Spain
- Morocco
- Iran

GROUP C

- France
- Australia
- Peru
- Denmark

GROUP D

- Argentina
- Iceland
- Croatia
- Nigeria

GROUP E

- Brazil
- Switzerland
- Costa Rica
- Serbia

GROUP F

- Germany
- Mexico
- Sweden
- Korea Republic
  (South Korea)

GROUP G

- Belgium
- Panama
- Tunisia
- England

GROUP H

- Poland
- Senegal
- Colombia
- Japan

EUROPE (13)

Germany, Spain, England, France, Russia, Belgium, Croatia, Denmark, Iceland, Poland, Portugal, Serbia, Sweden, Switzerland

Europe's entry of 13 teams also includes Russia as the host country (which makes 14 in total).

GERMANY

A BRIEF TEAM HISTORY

World Cup titles: 4 (1954, 1974, 1990, 2014)

Germany leads all nations with four second-place finishes (1966, 1982, 1986, 2002). And they lead with four third-place finishes, as well (1934, 1970, 2006, 2010). The defending champs have a long legacy of winning.

When it comes to sports, especially in the world of soccer, Germany is often accused of being "too good," "unstoppable." With four World Cup titles, that's hard to disagree with.

Germany has everything to gain from a past rich with success, a past that gives them every opportunity to move forward into the future with the same consistent momentum. As a leader in world soccer, they've had some ups and downs, but they've managed to keep above water throughout their amazing journey.

In 1930, Germany didn't play in the World Cup. In 1934, they placed third overall. By 1938, they didn't get out of the early first stage. In 1950, they didn't compete. In 1954, with steady passing and firm organization, the Germans were led by coach Herberger and players, Fritz Walter and Helmut Rahn, to defeat the great Hungarians in the final, winning West Germany's first World Cup title. In group play, they had lost to Hungary by a score of 8-3, making the final (a 3-2 win) a great comeback in which they displayed some of the resolve German teams have been known for. This would be the start of a great run that separates them from the rest of the world, alongside elite company, including Brazil and Italy. By 1958, West Germany had reached fourth place in Sweden, and in 1962—in Chile—they were knocked out in the quarterfinals.

In 1966, after defeating the powerful USSR in the semifinals (which was a result of sound team structure aligned with individual technique combined with a long-distance shot from Beckenbauer), West Germany faced another WWII enemy in the final, taking on England at Wembley Stadium before a packed house. Only a generation after one of the most brutal and deadliest wars, the two teams made the memorable walk onto the field, side by side, amid dignitaries and royalty in the stands—a game for the ages. England would score a questionable goal by Geoff Hurst, as the ball hit the crossbar and then it went just over the line. Or did it? There wasn't any goal-line technology back then. According to the referees, it was a goal. (A similar moment would occur again in 2010 against England in the World Cup, but this time it went in Germany's favor.) Despite the controversy, the Germans came in second place, losing 4-2.

After defeating England in the quarterfinals of the 1970 World Cup, West Germany had redeemed themselves a little after 1966. But they lost to Italy by 4-3 in the semifinals before earning the third-place title after defeating Uruguay.

West Germany's consistency for advancing far in World Cup tournaments would pay off again in 1974 (they were the hosts that year) when they defeated the Netherlands in the final. With this win, West Germany was now a two-time trophy holder, staking their claim alongside the familiar company of Italy and Brazil as one of the top soccer-playing nations in the world.* In 1978, West Germany lost early to Austria, forcing the retirement of coach Schön.

The talented Germans made a comeback in 1982. After first losing to Algeria early on, they made their way to the semifinals, meeting France in a notorious showdown that displayed their resolve and perseverance. It was one of the great games of the tournament—and World Cup history—as the Germans filtered in effective dribbling (with a touch of artistic integrity from Breitner) mixed with solid passing and takeovers, displaying unified alacrity for implementing the right pass for any given situation in pursuit of perfection. The dramatic game—which involved a French player being carried off on a stretcher—ended in a shootout in favor of Germany. Unfortunately for the Germans, they'd see their rival, Italy, hoist the trophy for a third time in the final game.

The year 1986 represented another triumph, as West Germany made it to the final yet again, only to be defeated by Maradona—who arguably had the best overall performance in Cup history—and Argentina. Under the guidance of Coach Beckenbauer, the Germans made a great comeback, tying the game 2-2, both goals coming off of corner kicks, only to be outdone by a late through-pass from Maradona to Burruchaga, and the rest was history.

---

* In 1974, West Germany joined Uruguay and Italy after they had earned their second title. Brazil was out in front with three titles.

By 1990, if it wasn't clear to a layman already, West Germany was a soccer powerhouse. Finally, after sixteen years and two second-place finishes, they regained the title of world champions by defeating Argentina in a rematch, thanks to a penalty kick guided in by Brehme. Beckenbauer became the first player and coach to win the World Cup (as the Germans tied Italy and Brazil for three titles).

Following the collapse of the Berlin Wall in 1989 (demolition began in June 1990 and finished in 1992), West Germany was reunited with East Germany. However, as things played out, the familiar title of West Germany was used in the 1990 World Cup, and, later, they were simply known as Germany in the 1994 World Cup and beyond.

The high standards of the German team proved not to be enough, however, in 1994 and 1998. They suffered an unexpected defeat in '94 to Bulgaria, led by Stoichkov, the Ballon d'Or winner of that year, and had a disappointing result in '98 after losing to Croatia 3-0 in the quarterfinals. By this time, many Germans were used to meeting high expectations, so they were very disappointed with their performances in the late 90s and early 2000s.

Things were back on track in 2002 when Germany made it to the finals, but they lost to a very talented Brazilian side. Where most countries in the world would've been happy with getting second place, many Germans continued to feel that just getting to the finals wasn't enough (much like how Brazilians approach each tournament). It would take a little time, but they'd get there.

In 2006, they lost in the semifinals; in 2010, they again lost in the semifinals; and, in 2014, they won the whole thing, making it the fourth time in their history.

In 2014, with Kroos, Özil, Müller, and Neuer, Germany presented a strong team that beat Brazil 7-1 in the semifinals, followed by a 1-0 win over Argentina in the final, and they're bringing a lot of the same to Russia 2018.

Germany has had a lot of semifinal appearances, second-place finishes, and actual World Cup titles. Not only that, but they also boast two players at the top of the list for the best World Cup scorers of all time: Gerd Muller with 14 goals (two ahead of Pelé) and Miroslav Klose with 16 goals.*

The Germans feel as though they can win the World Cup every time. They never settle; they're always looking ahead, yearning for more, staying ahead of the pack. They've been doing this for ages, not just for the World Cup, but also for the European Cup.

EUROPEAN CUP

Staying consistent with their World Cup dominance, the Germans won the illustrious European Cup[1] in 1972, 1980 and 1996. The German team translates all that experience from the European Cup to where it matters—every four years in the World Cup.

As of 2017, Germany placed first in the Confederations Cup held in Russia.

---

* As of 2014, Klose held the World Cup record with 16 goals.

FACTS ABOUT THEIR COUNTRY

Germany—land of Mercedes, BMW, adidas, and Puma—has a population of about 82 million and a GDP of approximately 3.3 trillion.[2]

Soccer is an integral part of the culture, and Germans take pride in their many achievements.

Lothar Matthäus leads German players in caps (which is soccer slang for an appearance in a national team game) with 150. He also leads the world in having played in the most World Cup games with 25. Miroslav Klose leads all German players with 71 goals. Klose is also the leading scorer in World Cups with 16 goals. And, he's right behind Matthäus for World Cup games played with 24. Harald Schumacher won goalie of the tournament at the 1986 World Cup. Oliver Kahn took the honor in 2002, and Manuel Neuer won it in 2014. Going into the 2018 World Cup, Germany's top three scorers are Miroslav Klose (71), Gerd Muller (68), and Lukas Podolski (49).

In 2014, Germany was the first European team to win the World Cup on South American soil.

Germans consume many different foods, beers (especially the beers, which the fans drink while cheering on their team), and wines. It's a diverse country with both industrial cities like Kassel and Hanover and beautiful countryside in the north, around the forests of Berlin, and to the south where tourists enjoy the mountain ranges of Bavaria.

WHERE THE TEAM IS TODAY—TACTICS AND STRATEGIES

The brilliant Germans have a strong team yet again. Defensively, the Germans stop opponents with well-organized team shape and individual talent.

Germany's formation may change during a game when transitioning from defense to offense; they will send different players into the attack, a strategy many, if not all, teams implement. Whether in a 4-3-3 or a 4-2-3-1 (two formations they've used in the past), the current German team has been known for exceptional passing. Compared with most teams in the world, they—along with Spain, the Netherlands, Brazil, and a few others—seem to have a better understanding of how the game should flow. They display a systematic approach to possession, connecting passes with a certain panache, a deft touch, a unique understanding of rhythm and timing. (See appendix under Germany, "Attention to Detail and Possession Passing" for bonus material.)

When the German team of 2014 was playing with a certain fluidity, with all passes lyrically linking together, it wasn't by mistake. It was part of a conceded effort by past players and coaches who evaluated what had previously worked and then combined that with new trends in the game—such as the means to dominate possession, as exemplified by teams like FC Barcelona. They then applied these successful strategies to each new German team. This approach has allowed for a better transition into the future and is why Germany enters Russia 2018 as one of the heavy favorites.

JOACHIM LÖW—A BRIEF COACHING PORTRAIT

Coach Joachim Löw brings a vast amount of experience to the team. As a player, he joined an assortment of teams, starting with the German side, SC Freiburg, in 1978 and ending with the Swiss team, FC Frauenfeld, in 1994.

From 1994-2004, Löw coached various club teams, including Stuttgart. Then, from 2004-2006, he became Germany's assistant coach under Jürgen Klinsmann. By 2006, he had taken over as Germany's head coach and guided them to their World Cup victory in 2014.

Player placement on the field is never by coincidence, either. Löw—who is calm and wise like a German Buddha—has guided the German team with a deft awareness of talent and chemistry between players based on a vision he has from a consortium of players and schemes from times of yore; this insight has guided a finished product—which has been, more or less, a group of players that emerged on the scene from 2006-2010, including Lahm, Schweinsteiger, Podolski, Müller, and others—which has been proven nothing short of brilliant. As older players get less playing time, their contributions carry over to the next generation. And Löw has made sure of this.

Sometimes a player makes a team only because certain decision-makers think that he's good in terms of the traditional "good body" test: "...the guy's an athlete, big, fast..." In other words, the player in question may look the part and may act the part, but inevitably he cannot play the part. Germany often avoids these kinds of mistakes. Most German players are chosen because they can "play chess at a high level," so to speak. By eliminating the "good body" types and focusing on soccer-smart players, teams like Germany—and Spain for that matter—have found the right pieces for the chessboard, which, theoretically, if guided the right way by the coach when lined up against other pieces on the board, bring long-term success.

This has been the case with the vision of Joachim Löw, both in the fine-tuned approach to passing—with an emphasis on fluid possession—and the players he has placed in certain positions to carry out the game plan...on their quest to repeat as champions.

KEY PLAYERS AND THEIR CHARACTERISTICS

Kroos, Özil, Müller, and Neuer

Definitely keep an eye out for Toni Kroos controlling the midfield with intelligent passing that strings together each side of the field. He is the conductor of possession seeing as how Germany plays the ball across the field from one outside player to another (be it an outside mid or defender). During stints of possession in their opponent's half, Kroos often likes to stand on the left side of the field, somewhat diagonal to the corner of the penalty box—similar to how Ronaldinho did toward the end of his career. From there he dictates the playing pace. In this situation, some teams fail to keep a man on him, allowing him to make intriguing additions to the swing of passing, which can often lead to strong scoring opportunities.

Helping Kroos in this midfield effort will be Mesut Özil (who tends to favor his left foot), applying skillful grace to each pass. Özil, in counterattacks, has an uncanny feel for the right pass at the right moment, which can be debilitating for opponents.

After bursting onto the scene in the 2010 World Cup, Müller has proven to be a unique goal-scorer and playmaker. Despite his lanky and skinny build, he has the ability to make the right pass for the moment, whether it be a simple touch to continue possession or a well-placed through-ball, and he always seems to serve it at just the right moment. This skill often goes unnoticed, but it is vital in Germany's success in a ninety-minute game.

In goal is the ever-talented Manuel Neuer, applying not only his dominate goal-keeping skills—some say the best in the world—but also his eager array of talent as a sweeper. Often he comes off his line to clear out danger or add to the possession game by distributing the ball (sometimes in tight spaces, which makes television announcers flinch) from defender to defender.

KEY PLAYER STATS*

	Games Played	Goals	Scoring Percentage
Kroos	79	12	15%
Özil	86	22	25%
Müller	89	37	41%
Neuer	74	0	0%

---

* For all teams, the Key Player Stats are current circa the publication of this book. They reflect each player's national team experience and a part of their contribution to the game.

WHAT TO WATCH FOR ON TV—HOW MESSI, NEYMAR, KROOS, AND OTHERS PLAY

Neuer should make the big saves, though he will probably prevent many scoring chances by coming off his line frequently. Also, his contribution as a sweeper-keeper helps establish possession for the key players in front of him.

Kroos, Özil, and Müller will help lead the team forward with passing and setting up effective dribbling opportunities for teammates. The Germans aren't often mentioned for their dribbling, but they use the skill quite well,* and often, with great effect, and this is thanks to their dominant passing ability, which allows for better opportunities to dribble. When the counterattack isn't on, the German players will begin systematically possessing the ball across the field with short passing combinations, usually orchestrated by Kroos, with the help of technically sound defenders and smart playing by Özil and Müller as well as the remaining world-class players. This is when the other team should be nervous. (See appendix under Germany, "German Soccer Moving Forward," for bonus material.)

As defending champions, Germany wants to be part of history as the first team to win two consecutive World Cups since Brazil in 1958 and 1962. So, whether they admit it or not, Russia 2018 is a landmark opportunity for them.

Overall team rating as defending champs under Coach Löw with a strong roster: 10

---

* Quite well, as in proper technique.

SPAIN

A BRIEF TEAM HISTORY

World Cup titles: 1 (2010)

HARD TO FIND SUCCESS...

During the years leading up to the 2010 World Cup in South Africa, Spain's journey was not without heartache. Their efforts read like a laundry list of complete World Cup failures. (See appendix under Spain, "They Were Always Good," for bonus material.)

Spain wasn't in the 1930 World Cup. In 1934, they were defeated in the quarterfinals. They didn't play in 1938. In 1950, they took fourth place, which isn't half bad but instead of following up with a strong contingent four years later, they didn't even qualify in 1954 or 1958. Then, in 1962 and 1966, they were eliminated in group play. Yet again, in 1970 and 1974, they didn't even qualify for either World Cup. In 1978, they were knocked out in the group stage.

Yet, despite World Cup failure, Spain's quality was evident. They possessed skillful players (including defenders) who made a lot of quick, short passes, often with the outside of the foot, indicating a certain flair for how they viewed the game.

At least they had won the 1964 European Cup, a huge accomplishment and something to build on.

As Miguel Angel Violan says in *Pep Guardiola: The Philosophy That Changed the Game*, "Success in sports comes and goes. What doesn't work one day can be effective the next. That is how things are in sports. The current situation and other circumstances have an influence, and of course it also has something to do with luck."[3] In Spain's case, they'd have to wait a few more years for their situation to drastically take a turn for the better.

Following Argentina in 1978 was a string of ongoing World Cup disappointment. In 1982, as the host nation, they were eliminated in the second group stage, but made up for it in 1986 when they finally made it to the quarterfinals, only to be knocked out in the round of 16 in 1990. By 1994, they again earned their way to the quarterfinals; in 1998, though, they were eliminated in the group stage. In 2002, they thought *maybe we'll make a better run at it*, only to be tossed out in the quarterfinals, and, yet again, in 2006, they couldn't make it past the group stage.

Frankly, on paper, with this lousy record, who could've imagined the reign of dominance from 2008 to 2012? Like they said in *Monty Python*: "Nobody expects the Spanish Inquisition!"

Despite the obvious inclination to dismiss Spain as a team that couldn't win the big tournament, they weren't giving up. Since 2006, something has been brewing in Spain, and given their proclivity for early departures from the World Cup, no one could've guessed that a small-sized group of overpassing, ultra-fastidious, possession-oriented players, largely from Barcelona, could carry the weight of the world over three major championships in a row.

In 2010, Spain finally won the World Cup. Outside of a loss to Switzerland, they appeared unstoppable.

The style they incorporated, the much-discussed Tiki-Taka,[4] was perfect for them. It wasn't just Iniesta and Xavi. It was the talented, skillful defenders that enabled Xavi and Iniesta to possess the ball so well. The defenders—including but not limited to Piqué, Sergio Busquets, Puyol, and Ramos—were so in tune with proper technique, the right pass for the right moment, while eagerly wanting the ball, that they pushed themselves to new heights. Their offensive understanding of the game allowed the play to flow through them, then through Xavi and Iniesta, along with Alonso, Pedro, Silva, Villa, and others. The back four had an in-depth understanding of possession which was reminiscent of classic German teams that took passing to a new level. (The German squads of the early 1990s with Hässler, Littbarski, and Matthäus were nothing without Augenthaler, Brehme, Kohler, and Berthold.)

The Golden Generation* was setting the example for how to play. The 2010 World Cup was the pinnacle, caught in between the dream-come-true Euro Cup performances of 2008 and 2012. After Spain defeated the Netherlands in the final game, they won their first World Cup title.

---

* The Golden Generation refers to Spain's victories at the 2008 Euro Cup, the 2010 World Cup, and the 2012 Euro Cup. Many of the same players were present for all three titles.

Two years later, Spain would win the Euro Cup 2012, achieving something that no other European team had ever done: winning the European Cup (2008), World Cup (2010), and European Cup (2012) in a row—The Triple. It was a remarkable run, similar to the Chicago Bull's back-to-back three-peats, Usain Bolt's three-for-three 100-meter golds, or the medal tally of Michael Phelps. Largely speaking, Spain's style and the success that came from it were due to defenders who knew *how* to incorporate everything so that the midfielders *could* incorporate everything.

The Triple (the three titles of the Golden Generation) represents the best passing teams of all time, and arguably the greatest three teams of all time. You could've hypothetically scattered those players throughout Spanish soccer history, and they would've all been standout performers, but to have all of them together at the same time, considering how they complimented one another, is amazing. They were the right players for the right time with the right coaching. Any team that follows will find it difficult to live up to those elite standards.

By the time the 2014 World Cup came around, the six-year parade was over, and Spain was slowing down. In a group with the Netherlands, Chile, and Australia, Spain failed to advance, and they left Brazil in utter disappointment.

EUROPEAN CUP

Spain won the European Cup in 1964, 2008, and 2012.

Historically, compared to some of their overachieving European neighbors, Spain has had a limited relationship with success.

In 1964—thirty years after Italy won their first World Cup and ten years after West Germany got their debut trophy—Spain won the European Cup on home soil, defeating the USSR with goals from Pereda and Marcelino. And, realistically, over forty years of nothing followed.

In between 1964 and 1990, Spain would have to watch as West Germany went on to win two more World Cups; Italy snuck a title in; the Netherlands made two World Cup finals and won the European Cup; and even France—who, until the 1970s, wasn't considered much of anything—won the European Cup.

Then, by 2000, France won the World Cup and another European Cup, and, in 2006, Italy would win yet another World Cup. Spain got nothing.

Finally, in 2008, Spain captured the European Cup of nations for the second time, defeating Germany in the final. Then in 2012, they repeated as European champions, overcoming Italy in the final.

FACTS ABOUT THEIR COUNTRY

Spain—the land of cathedrals, backpackers and great wine—as around 46 million people, and an estimated GDP of 1.2 trillion.

Essentially, *Frommer's*, a travel guidebook, would tell you it is common for Spaniards to begin the morning with a cup of coffee, often a cafe con leche, which contains half-coffee and half-milk, or a cortado, which contains a shot of espresso with a little milk.

Despite what they may or may not drink in the mornings, the one thing many Spaniards love with any meal is to talk about soccer. For watching games on TV, Spanish fans have many beers to choose from, including Estrella Galicia.

David Villa is the top Spanish scorer with 59 goals.

WHERE THE TEAM IS TODAY—TACTICS AND STRATEGIES

The technically sound Spanish coasted through the 2018 World Cup qualifications.

Using the success of the past, and likely staying with a 4-3-3 formation, Spain has been holding on to Iniesta and Ramos in an attempt to keep the train moving forward. The players reflect the same Tiki-Taka approach, though it might be considered Tiki-Taka Lite.

Frankly, it's been difficult to duplicate what once was. The Spanish players of World Cup Russia are of the highest caliber—their technique, passing, and knowledge of the game is beyond good—but they're going to have a difficult time finishing goals against the prowess of Germany, Argentina, and Brazil. Even though Spain remains in high company, they're falling off a bit, which was evident in Euro 2016. They're possibly returning to the Spain of old: a high-quality team that has a hard time in big tournaments. In their transition to new talent, Spain is still a dominant force, but they are not expected to take over Russia as they did in South Africa.

JULEN LOPETEGUI—A BRIEF COACHING PORTRAIT

The former goalie, Julen Lopetegui, took the lead as Spain's coach in 2016, replacing the great Vicente del Bosque.

As a player, he stood in goal for a few teams, including Real Madrid, Barcelona, and one game with Spain in 1994. As coach, his goal is to keep the passing machine moving forward while instituting a fresh crop of goal-scorers. The latter will be his biggest challenge.

KEY PLAYERS AND THEIR CHARACTERISTICS

David Silva, Isco, and Sergio Ramos

David Silva brings veteran leadership to the midfield as a holdover from the Golden Generation. He's a savvy passer with crafty dribbling ability. He plays well in tight spaces, which should help Spain in possession around their opponent's goal.

Isco will be a leading force in the midfield. He's a steady young talent who exudes quality in the possession game. He's displayed the passing connectivity that's hard to find for the central midfield position. He has a rare ability to pass the ball softly and early, setting up his teammates with just the right ball, similar to how Valderrama and Xavi did in their prime.

Sergio Ramos has moved from the outside defender position to that of an inside defender—the same role held by his former teammate, Puyol. Ramos is probably better suited as an outside defender, where he brought speed, toughness, aggression, and smart play. Though he still brings a positive list of attributes to the table. With his experience at Real Madrid—and, of course, with Spain—he creates a culture of winning.

KEY PLAYER STATS

	Games Played	Goals	Scoring Percentage
David Silva	116	33	28%
Isco	24	7	29%
Sergio Ramos	147	11	7%

WHAT TO WATCH FOR ON TV—HOW MESSI, NEYMAR, KROOS, AND OTHERS PLAY

When it comes to Spain, team passing is more important than any one player.

Spain usually puts forth great individual talent that exudes a team philosophy. There won't be too many—if any—flashy players, demanding the ball, attention, and self-serving gratification of being in the limelight. In this respect, Spain is similar to Germany. They don't have star players who must have the ball at their feet to get the whole team going. All of Spain's players need the ball for the unit to succeed.

Watch for the short passing while the players move the ball through numerous channels in a unique fashion which is a focal point of the Tiki-Taka style and still Spain's basic approach to the game. (Within the Tiki-Taka approach, often two players will exchange multiple passes, improving possession and chemistry within the passing structure, which, over the course of a ninety-minute game, wears down the resolve of the opposing team. It also creates better scoring opportunities. This is where its effectiveness gets tricky. The Golden Generation had a unique understanding of Tiki-Taka, which makes them a tough group to live up to.)

The origins of Spain's style, of course, come from the influence of the Dutch player and coach, Johan Cruyff. The style had continued to progress at Barcelona under the guidance of coaches Louis van Gaal and Frank Rijkaard before trickling over to the Spanish national team. It was later adopted by Spanish coaches, including Vicente del Bosque, the coach of Spain from 2008-2016. The Dutch vision sought to implement this style of play within the youth systems, notably the Barcelona La Masia youth academy, which had similarities with the youth academies of Ajax in the Netherlands. At La Masia, various players were educated in this system, including Iniesta and Pedro. Spain and Barcelona definitely benefited from this training made available to the young players, players who turned into adults and eventually took over the responsibility of leading their teams on the field. In Russia 2018, many of the Spanish players will bring this influence to each game.[5]

Without a doubt, Spain in Russia 2018 will provide high quality, but actually scoring goals will be another question altogether.

Overall Team Rating: 9

ENGLAND

A BRIEF TEAM HISTORY

World Cup titles: 1 (1966)

The English are truly unique. The steady, ready, and soon-to-be champs again are a country with so much history in the greatest game.

Like a few other top teams in the world—such as Germany, Italy, and Brazil—the English deserve an extended conversation for a few reasons: They invented the game. They have one of the world's best professional leagues. They won the World Cup once, and since that time (1966) things have not been good for their national team in the World Cup. The mystery of England's early departures from World Cups is an ongoing fascination with people around the world—a mystery even Sherlock Holmes might not be able to solve.

When it comes down to it, something has always been off—an injury, bad chemistry on the field, a problem with the referee, someone cheated, or just bad luck. Keegan was injured; Maradona used his hand; Lampard's shot crossed the line! England's

World Cup adventure has been a crazy, interesting, exciting, disappointing, and emotional ride, to say the least.

In most cases, no matter what the competition, English teams will have an advantage to win based on talent, high-quality training, experience, and tradition. But, as we will see, World Cups have not been kind to England for a long time.

Before the modern era, England, under the Football Association (FA), declined to play in the World Cups of 1930, 1934, and 1938. After all, what was the World Cup back then? Minus the prestige it has today, one might understand how England opted to say thanks, but no thanks. In 1930, with travel being somewhat of a hassle, Uruguay was way down in the Southern Hemisphere. So, possibly, they were being lazy. Then, in 1934, the competition was held in Italy under the guidance and influence of Mussolini, who was eventually accused of being influential in fixing the tournament in Italy's favor. Possibly, they had a feeling about that Mussolini fellow. Just prior to WWII, France, who was England's old rival, hosted in 1938, another easy reason for the English to decline.

By the end of WWII, Brazil hosted the first post-WWII World Cup in 1950, which England agreed to join. It wasn't the best showing for them, placing 8th overall, taking an embarrassing defeat from the United States.

In 1954, after tying Belgium, 4-4, and defeating the hosts Switzerland, 2-0, in the group stage, England progressed to the elimination phase, losing 4-2 to Uruguay at the St. Jakob Stadium in Basel, Switzerland. The next let down happened in 1958, this time in Sweden. England tied their first game against the Soviet Union, 2-2, followed by a 0-0 tie against eventual tournament champions, Brazil. There next match ended in another 2-2 tie against Austria, leading to a playoff against the USSR, which England lost, 1-0, and they were eliminated from the tournament.

In 1962, England finished second in their group—which included Bulgaria, Argentina, and Hungary—with a win, loss, and a draw, thanks to goals from Flowers, Charlton, and Greaves. In the quarterfinals against Brazil, their goal by Gerry Hitchens wasn't enough, and they lost, 3-1.

Prior to 1966, their golden year, things were clearly disappointing and somewhat competitive. They had something to build on, though. As the host nation, the 1966 World Cup opened the door for England to make their stand, which they did, winning their group with two wins and one draw (defeating Mexico and France and tying with Uruguay) before overtaking Argentina 1-0 in the quarters, followed by a 2-1 win over Portugal in the semis. They earned the title of world champions by defeating their heated rival, West Germany, 4-2. All matches for England were played in Wembley Stadium, which served as a massive advantage for the home side. This was it, England's great triumph. They took on the world and reminded everyone how superior they were, or ought to be.

In the post-1966 era, England has dramatically come up short in World Cups, notably 1986, with "the hand of God"* and

---

* Maradona's first of two goals against England in the 1986 World Cup, which he scored illegally with his hand.

2010, with the "ball crossing the line"* against Germany. But, before 1986 rolled around, there were four other tournaments to endure.

In 1970, as defending champs, they emerged second overall in their group with a 1-0 win over Romania thanks to a goal from Geoff Hurst, a close loss to Brazil, and a 1-0 win over Czechoslovakia with a goal from Allan Clarke. Though, they lost right away, 3-2, against West Germany in the quarterfinals after starting out at a 2-0 lead with goals from Alan Mullery and Martin Peters. 1974 and 1978, though, were not good years, as England failed to qualify.

In 1982, following three wins in group play against France, Czechoslovakia, and Kuwait, England advanced in a tournament based on round-robin play, wherein England drew 0-0 with West Germany, followed by another 0-0 tie with Spain, sending West Germany to the next round.

In 1986, with a win, draw, and a loss in a group with Morocco, Poland, and Portugal, England moved onto the second round, defeating Paraguay, 3-0, with goals from Gary Lineker and Peter Beardsley. Then, of course, came the famous loss to Argentina in front of over 100,000 people in which Diego Maradona sprung into the air and swatted the ball with his hand over the reach of goalkeeper, Peter Shilton, for the first goal. It happened so quickly that it looked like Maradona headed the ball, and the referee missed it. This was followed by arguably the greatest single goal in World Cup history, where Maradona gallantly

---

* Lampard's legitimate goal against Germany in the 2010 World Cup which was disallowed.

dribbled half the field past multiple English defenders, who seemed to be jogging alongside him, and passed Shilton for the goal. Lineker knocked in the last goal, heading in a cross from Barnes, only to see England eliminated once again.

The Italian jaunt of 1990 represented a great tournament for England. They left their group stage with a win and two draws against Ireland, the Netherlands, and Egypt with goals from Lineker and Mark Wright. In the second round, David Platt scored the winner against Belgium, placing them up against the upstarts, Cameroon, in the quarterfinals—a place no one anticipated Cameroon would be in. In one of the most exciting games of the tournament, England scored first with Platt before falling behind, 2-1, with goals from Cameroon players Emmanuél Kunde and Eugène Ekéké, along with some great creative play from Cameroonian legend, Roger Milla, who contributed off the bench. It would have been World Cup history, the first African team making it to the semifinals, if not for two late penalties from Lineker, the first arriving toward the end of the game in the eighty-third minute. Back on top, it seemed, and ready for the next challenge, England entered the semis against the much-favored West German side—a game which ended in a draw and was decided by penalty kicks. Lineker, Beardsley, and Platt scored the first three, followed by two misses from Stuart Pearce and Chris Waddle. The Germans won the shootout after Andreas Brehme, Lothar Matthäus, Karl-Heinz Riedle, and Olaf Thon scored each of their kicks.

As it turned out, 1994 was another "what in the world happened" year for England, as they failed to qualify. And, a year earlier, in 1993, they lost to the US by a surprising score of 2-0 in the US Cup held at Foxborough Stadium in Boston, the sight of the

Boston Tea Party of 1773. England had been caught off-guard yet again. But in the soccer game of 1993, none of the American players were disguised as Native Americans—that would've been in poor taste, not to mention a uniform violation, going against the rules and regulations of the Ethics Committee of FIFA (so one would think, anyway).

The World Cup of 1998 was a year of change, or so it was thought. Along with flashy play from newcomer, Michael Owen (who would eventually be voted winner of the Ballon d'Or in 2001), England also had an arsenal of talent comprised of Alan Shearer, David Beckham, Paul Ince, Le Saux, and Paul Scholes (who had always been a very underappreciated talent). Upon leaving their group—with two wins over Colombia and Tunisia, and a loss to Romania—England found themselves in an epic showdown with a stacked Argentinean side, featuring Ortega and Veron. It was an exciting game, with a great goal from Owen, showing his explosive speed when he dashed away from the last defender and chipped a line drive past the keeper. Though, it wasn't meant to be, and England lost in a shootout. Back to the drawing board.

In 2002, England got out of their group—which included Sweden, Argentina, and Nigeria—with a win and two draws. In the second round, they defeated Denmark, setting up a quarterfinal match with Brazil, the eventual champions. Again, England played well, but luck wasn't on their side.

Looking back, 2006 was still hopeful. England led their group— Sweden, Paraguay, and Trinidad and Tobago—with two wins and a draw. In the second round, England defeated Ecuador with a goal from Beckham, which led to a quarterfinal loss to Luis

Figo, C. Ronaldo, and Portugal. It went down to penalties with misses from Lampard, Gerrard, and Carragher, with the only goal coming from Hargreaves.

All in all, 2010 represents one of the more frustrating outings for England, in almost every sense possible. They started things out having to endure reminders about their first opponent, the United States, and their past defeats, particularly the loss in 1950. By way of Gerrard, England scored first, and pubs around the island went mental, only to have the game tied from an innocent looking shot from outside the box off the foot of Clint Dempsey. As the ball rolled toward Robert Green, half the population of the British Isles could've gotten up for a drink in the kitchen only to return to find that the shot was still on route to the keeper. Then, mysteriously, the ball went off the goalie's gloves and over the line for a goal. Part one of their disappointment. Following with a tie against Algeria and a win over Slovenia, England placed second in their group (a group won by the United States; "How did that happen?" most people of England had to have wondered). The next stop was Germany in the second round. England had played robotically in previous games, not getting the most out of their star forward, Wayne Rooney. Germany went ahead by two goals in the first half. Then, following a score from Matthew Upson, the tide was turning in England's favor; you could feel the momentum changing. They were playing better; something clicked; they were less robotic. Something magical was about to happen. Something was in the air, and then it happened: Lampard's—legitimate—game-tying goal hit the crossbar and went over the line, but the referees didn't see in real-time what instant replay showed to be a clear and decisive goal. This would've tied the game going into halftime, and who knows what could've taken place from there. Unfortunately, for

England, Germany went ahead and won, 4-1, taking advantage of England's misfortune.

The 2014 World Cup wasn't any better for English morale, as the Three Lions got two losses and one draw (with fellow competitors Costa Rica, Uruguay, and Italy), which was not enough to advance into the second round. This left them 48 years removed from 1966, with their heads down, thinking better luck next time.

Perhaps all these epic moments in England's World Cup history provide a small window into the agony of defeats and help to explain how England has been tormented with failure for years. To many observers, their style hasn't changed much, with results essentially remaining the same. Yet, they're always relevant as a world-class team.

EUROPEAN CUP

If England's World Cup experience has been up and down, things have been outright terrible for their European Cup record.

Considering the European Cup, which many people believe to be more competitive than the actual World Cup (a theory based simply on there being more competitive teams in one region, while excluding less talented teams from Asia or CONCACAF, for instance), England hasn't even made it to the finals. Not once. Zero appearances. Not even a second-place finish. From 1960 onward, the European Cup was taken by the following teams: the Soviet Union, Spain, Italy, West Germany, Czechoslovakia, West Germany, France, the Netherlands, Denmark, Germany,

France, Greece, Spain, Spain, and Portugal. But not England, the inventors of the game.

Both the European Cup and World Cup represent a fraction of the disappointment for the English. But, each year, they prepare as if they're destined to take it all. (See appendix under England, "England's Intriguing Dilemma," for bonus material.)

FACTS ABOUT THEIR COUNTRY

England is famously known for inventing soccer in the mid-1800s. It came together as an offshoot of rudimentary forms of rugby. Modern-day England has a population of around 54 million, and a GDP of approximately 2.3 trillion.

Wayne Rooney—who is still charging forward—is England's leading scorer with over 50 goals. In second place is Bobby Charlton (1958-1970) with 49. Behind him, in third place, is Gary Lineker with 48.

While watching games on TV, people in England have many beers to choose from, including Late Knights Worm Catcher, Harvey's Blue Label, and Fuller's London Porter.

WHERE THE TEAM IS TODAY—TACTICS AND STRATEGIES

At times, England can be exciting to watch. Everyone around the world knows they're great tacklers. This cannot be refuted. As

Diego Maradona has said, they play hard and they're honorable as well; you won't get too many cheap shots from an English player. They play with great sportsmanship.

There's something electric about England taking the field. It's a common axiom that they bring the emotion and create a fast-paced game. Because of great players from the past, like Robson, Waddle, Gascoigne, Barnes, Fowler, Owens, Scholes, Gerrard, and Rooney, it's assumed that if all those guys were together, magic could happen. The problem is that it's hard to catch all those guys at the same time, and then you have to hope and pray they have the right chemistry together.

Using the talent at their disposal, which is always top tier, the English approach to soccer for years has been direct and to *possess the ball with purpose* on the field, attacking down the line. This year's team, which will likely be in a 4-4-2 formation, is no different. And they are expecting a big result. (See appendix under England, "England's Interesting Approach Down the Line," for bonus material.)

GARETH SOUTHGATE—A BRIEF COACHING PORTRAIT

As of 2016, Gareth Southgate signed a four-year agreement to coach England into the World Cup. In taking the job, he accepted all the pressure in the world, and he's determined to give England the best chance possible to make up for lost time.

Born in 1970, Southgate's professional career (1988-2006) was spent playing with Crystal Palace, Aston Villa, and Middlesbrough.

He also served as a longstanding member of the national team from 1995-2004, making 57 appearances.

His philosophy involves using strikers and outside midfielders down the line, crossing the ball—with proper service—from the wings with a firm backline that also has the aerial capability to stomp out opposing corner kicks, while serving as an asset on the offensive side of free kicks.

Under the fresh influence of England's new coach, their prospects are looking good.

KEY PLAYERS AND THEIR CHARACTERISTICS

Wayne Rooney, Daniel Sturridge, and Marcus Rashford

Wayne Rooney brings a veteran presence with an all-around game that will lead England in the right direction. He was once a goal-scoring phenom of a forward, now converted to a central midfield role. His keen sense of awareness guides the team with smart passing and pivotal episodes of dribbling.

Daniel Sturridge is a newcomer with a great sense for goal. Watch for his ability to break free from defenders, creating strong scoring opportunities.

Marcus Rashford is a young talent that England is depending upon for many scoring chances. He's fast and has a knack for getting behind defenders with good dribbling or a darting run to receive a through-ball.

KEY PLAYER STATS

	Games Played	Goals	Scoring Percentage
Rooney	119	53	44%
Sturridge	26	8	30%
Rashford	13	2	15%

WHAT TO WATCH FOR ON TV—HOW MESSI, NEYMAR, KROOS, AND OTHERS PLAY

England likes to play the counterattack with a lot of speed, and telling, crisp passes. For 2018, they have very capable forwards and wingers who can carry this out; they're fast, aggressive, skillful, and determined to put England back on the map—a dangerous combination for their opponents.

England will provide an aerial threat from all set pieces, including free kicks from the wings as well as corners. Keep an eye on their tall, strong defenders that get into the box, muscling for position to knock in a goal or two. Their outside defenders are like marathon runners on both sides of the ball. Given their experience, combined with new talent, they should be a competitive team with potential to go far into the elimination rounds.

Overall Team Rating: 8, leaning toward 8.5

FRANCE

A BRIEF TEAM HISTORY

World Cup titles: 1 (1998)

The flamboyant and entertaining French essentially took off with soccer in the late 1970s. In the early days, France had a tepid, on-again, off-again relationship with the World Cup.

In the 1930 World Cup, France didn't get past the group stage; in 1934, they lost in the opening round; by 1938, they made the quarterfinals; then, in 1950, they didn't compete; and in 1954, they didn't get out of their group.

By 1958, in Sweden, things changed in a big way, as they placed third overall. But, in the next few years, things went back to subpar.

In 1962, France didn't make it through qualifications; in 1966, in England, they didn't get out of their group; in 1970 and 1974, they didn't make it through qualifications; and, in 1978, in Argentina, they didn't get out of their group.

With the rise of Michel Platini, who is regarded by many as the best French player of all time, along with a multitude of talent, including Giresse, Tigana, and Rochteau, France soared onto the map in a big way, placing fourth overall in the 1982 World Cup. They barely missed the final game, losing in a classic semifinal to West Germany—a game that is definitely on the top ten list of all time World Cup classics.

Returning with a similar lineup, France flourished in the 1986 World Cup. With the help of a subtle chip over the sliding keeper, Platini pushed France past Italy in the second round toward a showdown with Brazil—arguably another on the top ten list of all-time World Cup games. From the attack of Josimar, Junior, Muller, and Careca, Brazil took an early lead with a powerful goal from Careca that nearly broke the back of the net. Led by Socrates, the charge was on. Brazil was looking for more goals. Then, by way of a blunder in front of the Brazilian net and a possible foul on the goalie that was overlooked, Platini equalized, tapping the ball in from the far post. Zico, coming in as a substitute, had an opportunity to push Brazil ahead on a penalty kick, but it was saved by Joel Bats. In the penalty shootout, another unlikely miss occurred from Platini, as he sent his kick over the bar, on his birthday, no less. But France would prevail, moving ahead to a semifinal rematch with West Germany. Again, the Germans won, and France went on to earn a third-place finish over Belgium.

Generally speaking, until the 1970s, soccer took a backseat in French culture. Platini, along with the help of Giresse, Tigana, and others, helped elevate the game to higher levels, bringing a wider French audience to the festivities. All this momentum, however, left something to be desired, as France didn't qualify for World Cups 1990 and 1994.

Then, in 1998, as the host nation, they became world champions led by Zidane and Deschamps by defeating Brazil, 3-0, in the final. However, in the very next World Cup of 2002, France would disappoint big time, as they couldn't get out of their group.

For the 2006 World Cup, desperately wanting to make an impact, Zidane—who is in the conversation with Platini for best French player of all time—was leading the pack for one last go-around. In true form, with a dazzling display of defensive talent combined with an electric attack—which included Zidane, Ribery, and Henry—France got to the final and squared up against a determined Italian side. Possibly the most exciting championship game in World Cup history, an intense back-and-forth 1-1 draw went down to the wire, and, always considerate of public consumption and just to add a little more drama, Zidane was ejected for headbutting Italian defender Materazzi in the chest (allegedly, following comments about Zidane's sister). As things turned out, Italy won in a shootout.

World Cup 2010 continued with a dramatic touch for France, as the players united around a teammate who was sent home (based on words with the coach) and protested by not practicing. In disgust, one coach threw his whistle to the ground; tempers were flaring. Earning headlines around the world, the mutiny was led by Patrice Evra. The players resigned to a bus and shut the doors; the head coach was given a letter signed by the players, and they requested that he read it aloud—a classic showdown with authority, French style. The result was dismal, as France didn't get out of their group. A cynical headline could have read: *"Nous n'avons peut-etre pas gagne le tournoi, mais nous avons gagne quelque chose de plus grand aux yeux de la democratie!"*

In other words: "We may not have won the tournament, but we won something bigger in the eyes of democracy!"

At the 2014 World Cup in Brazil, the play on the field was better, but France didn't make it past the quarterfinals.

EUROPEAN CUP

In 1984, France won the European Cup for the first time—a huge accomplishment for French soccer. Following the 1998 World Cup, they were on a roll, winning the 2000 European Cup as well—a huge milestone.

At the 2016 European Cup final, hosted in France before a packed house, they came within inches of taking the crown of Europe back to France, only to be outdone by Portugal.

FACTS ABOUT THEIR COUNTRY

France—the land of phenomenal wine and cuisine—has a population of about 66.9 million people, with a GDP of around 2.4 trillion.

Karim Benzema and Olivier Giroud have cracked the top ten list for all-time scorers in France. Number one on the list is World Cup champion, Thierry Henry, with 51. Number two is European Cup champion, Michel Platini, with 41.

Platini, who some assert is France's all-time best player, flourished as the captain of his country's team during the 1970s and 80s. Yet, his last international game was in 1988, playing for

Kuwait; he played for a short time in a friendly against the USSR. Way to end on a strange note.

Though the French are known for world-class wine, a few beers that may populate soccer parties include Duyck Jenlain Ambree, La Choulette Blonde, and Kronenbourg 1664.

WHERE THE TEAM IS TODAY—TACTICS AND STRATEGIES

Coming off a second place finish at the 2016 European Cup, which they also hosted, France is in good form.

They'll likely go with a 4-3-3; though, they've used other formations in the past. Defensively, they close down opponents very well, swarming them and stifling attacks with athletic players who have good instincts.

In the attack, their dynamite lineup plays with calm fluidity, capitalizing on a structured passing system that, at times, straddles the flair of pickup soccer. Often, their play is brilliant, making them one of the most exciting teams to watch.

DIDIER DESCHAMPS—A BRIEF COACHING PORTRAIT

Didier Deschamps played midfield with a few different professional sides, including the likes of Nantes, Marseille, Bordeaux, Juventus, Chelsea, and Valencia. He was also a key member of the French championship team during the 1998 World Cup.

With such a talented group this year, Deschamps' task is to keep the chemistry in balance but still bring out each player's potential. His ideal means to accomplish this is to keep the short passing game intact, which France does very well. They exude confidence in tight spaces, looking to pass the ball within inches of their opponents' feet—a thing of beauty. If that isn't enough, they exploit open space extremely well in counterattacks with fluid passes that always seem to lead the next player forward with just the right amount of touch. Keeping the team on track with what they do well should be his biggest concern. That, and stressing the importance of patience in tight games.

KEY PLAYERS AND THEIR CHARACTERISTICS

Paul Pogba, Olivier Giroud, Dimitri Payet, and Antoine Griezmann

Pogba, a midfielder with Manchester United, is good in the air, at times handy with the dribble, a good athlete, and—according to some—way overvalued. He came up short as leader of France in the 2016 Euro. Though, despite some criticism, he's a good two-way player who French fans hope can lead France toward a better outcome in 2018.

Giroud, a tall forward, has been heavily criticized by many people in the French public, claiming he's inconsistent. But, depending on the moment, he's typically a threat, either on the ground or in the air. He's not particularly known for creating his own shot; rather, he relies on a sound French passing attack to put him in positions to succeed.

Payet, born in 1987, is an interesting midfielder who can break a game wide open, as he showed by his scoring ability in the 2016 Euro tournament. He was born on an island near Madagascar in the Indian Ocean in a French territory called Reunion. He's fine-tuned his skills there and in France. He's good on the dribble and elusive around the box, creating his own shot.

Griezmann, the left-footer, uses an all-around offensive game that is accentuated by crafty dribbling moves and accurately timed passes. Always in the right place, Griezmann has a knack for finding the back of the net in every way possible.

KEY PLAYER STATS

	Games Played	Goals	Scoring Percentage
Pogba	49	8	16%
Giroud	68	28	41%
Payet	37	8	21%
Griezmann	47	18	38%

WHAT TO WATCH FOR ON TV—HOW MESSI, NEYMAR, KROOS, AND OTHERS PLAY

Keep an eye on the free-flowing style of the French led by Pogba and Griezmann, who will be flanked by fast, talented, and energetic wing play on each side. The team plays a relaxed, aesthetically pleasing style, with probably the smoothest counterattacking transition in the tournament.

Overall Team Rating: 9

RUSSIA

A BRIEF TEAM HISTORY

For the World Cups prior to 1991, the USSR—which included Russia, the Ukraine, Belarus, Estonia, Latvia, and others—established the team that Russian players participated with.

Following the 1991 election of Boris Yeltsin, Russia-proper got their first World Cup experience in 1994, losing out in the group stage. Russia didn't qualify for World Cup 1998 in France. As for 2002, the Russians lost out again in group play. Things didn't come together as planned in 2006 or 2010, as Russia failed to qualify.

World Cup 2014 was a different story, as the Russians qualified for Brazil, but couldn't get out of their group. As the host nation in 2018, Russia is looking to have a strong showing, while also building on the experience for future World Cups.

EUROPEAN CUP

As for the European Cup,* between 1996 and 2016, Russia's best result was in 2008 when they reached the semifinals and eventually took third place overall.

---

* The USSR won the European Cup in 1960 and placed second in 1964, 1972, and 1988, while taking fourth place in 1968.

FACTS ABOUT THEIR COUNTRY

Russia, the vast, multi-cultured land with a rich history, has a population of approximately 144.5 million people and a GDP of around 1.4 trillion.

This is the first World Cup Russia has hosted. Since 1992, the Russian team has been sponsored by adidas, Reebok, Nike, and adidas again.

To date, the highest scorer in Russian history is Aleksandr Kerzhakov, who is also the only Russian player—as yet—to reach 30 goals.

Popular Russian beers that are sure to be around World Cup festivities are Baltika Number 8 (wheat), Baltika Number 9 (pale), and Ochakovo.

WHERE THE TEAM IS TODAY—TACTICS AND STRATEGIES

Around mid-March, 2017, a good year before the 2018 World Cup, Russia was ranked 60th in the world. For perspective, the United States was ranked 30th, while Argentina was number one. Russia's approach to the game comes across like the Netherlands meets Italy with a touch of Romania on a so-so outing. In backline possession, they make use of the goalie and the defenders who quickly work the ball between one another. They look to implement aggressive play down the lines. They force the issue. There's a fast pace, with a lot of passes "right at the player" and not much two-man game, or soft lead passes (which you find with the French and Spanish). Overall, with the absence of Andrey Arshavin, they are lacking in the department of creative play; flashy dribbling is virtually nonexistent. For this generation of players, there's a lot of quality and experience, but some criticism they've endured over recent years would be the absence of a guaranteed goal. Likely taking the field in a 4-4-2, they tend to play as if they're down a goal with twenty minutes left in the game. However, they can compete with anyone and win on any given day. It's not as though they're no good. They're a quality side, representing a nation that loves soccer, and, as hosts, passion should carry them a long way.

STANISLAV CHERCHESOV—A BRIEF COACHING PORTRAIT

Stanislav Cherchesov was a goalie and played from 1981-2002 with a variety of teams, including Spartak Moscow and Dynamo Dresden. From 1990-2000, he also had the unique opportunity to play for the Soviet Union (8 caps), CIS* (2 caps), and Russia (39 caps).

In 2016, he took over the job as Russia's coach with the goal of building the team for the 2018 World Cup—a large responsibility

---

* The CIS was an ephemeral and conditional national team of the Football Federation of the Soviet Union; as such, it represented the Common Wealth of Independent States during the transfer of government as the Soviet Union dissolved. (The Soviet Union had qualified for the European Cup in 1991, so a unified team—the CIS— was made to participate in Euro 1992, and after the tournament the Russian national team became its own entity.)

for anyone as host nation. With all eyes on his team's performance, he will be attempting to bring together a coalition of talent—many of whom play for Russian teams—that can not only stand on its own but also use the home crowd to its advantage, as Russia is hoping to make a big run.

Possession play is usually something a Russian team handles well in that their players have competent skill. Although, they have a tendency to push toward the goal quickly, which, at times, can take possession for granted. With that said, transforming good possession into goals is the task of the coaching staff under the guidance of Cherchesov. That challenge has prevented past Russian teams from moving forward into the deeper rounds of a World Cup. With a sound roster, Cherchesov and staff look to use possession to their advantage and capitalize on big moments in big games.

KEY PLAYERS AND THEIR CHARACTERISTICS

Artem Dzyuba, Yuri Zhirkov, Dmitri Kombarov, and Aleksandr Kokorin

Artem Dzyuba, a forward, joined Zenit Saint Petersburg in 2015. He's a tall player, who gets into the box well to knock in goals. His strong presence provides a good target for his teammates to test opposing defenses.

Yuri Zhirkov, born in 1983, is a veteran presence and can usually be found on the left side of the field, sparkling in the wing with crafty skill and intuitive passes.

Dmitri Kombarov, who has been with Russia since 2012, is a veteran defender—usually found outside on the left—who pushes his opponent for every inch of space, fighting for possession of the ball, and has the capability of providing a helping hand with some fine finishes, as evidenced from his time at Spartak Moscow.

Aleksandr Kokorin is a forward who's played with Russia since 2011. He provides an athletic and active presence up top as a capable finisher, while actively looking to set up teammates.

KEY PLAYER STATS

	Games Played	Goals	Scoring Percentage
Artem Dzyuba	22	11	50%
Yuri Zhirkov	79	2	2%
Dmitri Kombarov	45	2	4%
Aleksandr Kokorin	46	12	26%

WHAT TO WATCH FOR ON TV—HOW MESSI, NEYMAR, KROOS, AND OTHERS PLAY

Russian defenders challenge strong for defensive headers. Other teams can be sure of that. Collectively, the team provides a lot of high-paced action down the lines, searching for opportunities to reach the end line and to play the ball across the mouth of the goal. They're a solid team, yet, with somewhat limited possession play, they're always looking for that one, final, hero pass to set up a goal, which is usually an isolation pass to a forward at the top of the box with little support. With the crowd behind them to rally them forward, they could push past a few teams ranked higher in the FIFA hierarchy, and by the same token, they have the collective talent to go deep in the tournament.

Overall Team Rating: 7

With home field advantage, Russia's rating could easily be an 8.

BELGIUM

A BRIEF TEAM HISTORY

Belgium's early World Cup days were a struggle. For World Cups 1930, 1934, and 1938, Belgium couldn't get past the first round. They didn't compete in 1950. In 1954, they didn't get out of their group.

For World Cups 1958, 1962, and 1966, they didn't qualify. In 1970, they didn't get out of their group. For 1974 and 1978, they didn't qualify. By the 1980s, things were beginning to improve for old Belgium. In 1982, they made it to the second group phase.

World Cup Mexico, in 1986, represented their best year. In a group with Mexico, Paraguay, and Iraq, they managed to come in third, which advanced them to the second round where they faced the Soviet Union, winning 4-3. Their quarterfinal opponent was Spain, who they beat in penalty kicks. The championship was one game away. After years of dismal results, they were right there with a chance to win it all. Yet, Argentina and Maradona were too much, as Belgium lost in the semifinals and eventually surrendered the third-place title to France, taking fourth overall.

For 1990 and 1994, they got no farther than the round of 16. Things weren't too great in 1998, as they failed to get out of group play. They made the round of 16 in 2002. For 2006 and 2010, they didn't qualify.

Things were better in Brazil in 2014. With a strong team—which included De Bruyne and Eden Hazard—they made the quarterfinals.

Now they're on track with an exciting team, ready to make a run at Russia 2018.

FACTS ABOUT THEIR COUNTRY

Not quite as small as Luxemburg or Liechtenstein, Belgium's population is around 11 million people, with an estimated GDP of 470 billion.

Bernard Voorhoof and Paul Van Himst are Belgium's leading goal-scorers, tied with 30.

Where to start with Belgian beers? There are so many! Duvel, Vedett, and many others will make the rounds as Belgian fans congregate to watch their team on TV.

Many Belgians that travel or live outside their country find a way to watch their team in action. At Goal, a soccer bar in Los Angeles, on the beautiful West Coast of the United States, evidently, many Belgian soccer fans arrived en masse for games during the 2014 World Cup, ordering large quantities of Belgian beer. According to Jay, who works at Goal, when Belgium played the United States in the knockout round, "…it was as chaotic and awesome as I've ever seen this bar before." He added, "We sold more Stella and Palm than you can imagine. Mind blowing how much Palm and Stella we sold."

WHERE THE TEAM IS TODAY—TACTICS AND STRATEGIES

In recent years, Belgium has topped FIFA's charts as one of the best teams in the world. This is in large part thanks to the firepower of Eden Hazard and Kevin De Bruyne. Their presence and individual playmaking ability has pushed Belgium into the upper echelon of world-class teams. For now, they remain. But, as past years have shown, Belgium will be a team ranked somewhere in the top twenty or thirty.

On the whole, likely mobilizing with a 4-2-3-1 or a 4-4-2 (with a forward that drops back a bit on defense), Belgium resembles Spain intertwined with Colombia.

ROBERTO MARTINEZ—A BRIEF COACHING PORTRAIT

Roberto Martinez was coaching with Everton from 2013-2016 before he took over Belgium in 2016. He's coached a handful of teams, including Swansea City, Wigan Athletic, Everton, and Belgium.

Born in Spain, he was a defensive midfielder that played with a spell of teams, including Wigan Athletic and Swansea City.

His Spanish background is serving the Belgians well; he's implemented a passing structure that enables the stars plenty of room to do what they do best—go at defenders. And so far, under his guidance, the team has excelled through qualifications and looks very good for the future.

KEY PLAYERS AND THEIR CHARACTERISTICS

Jan Vertonghen, Eden Hazard, and Kevin De Bruyne

Jan Vertonghen is a veteran defender who is a confident, well-trained tackler with very good defensive and offensive skills; he's one of those defenders who calmly cleans up messes with a steady hand and has the ability to smartly dribble away from pressing forwards, and even midfielders, moving the ball into the attack. For a defender, his passing touch is excellent.

Eden Hazard is an attacking player—with professional experience at Lille and Chelsea—who dribbles extremely well, pushing the issue with defenses, keeping them off balance and creating scoring chances for his teammates and himself. In doing so, he's a dynamic goal-scorer and one of the tournament's top offensive players, with quickness, speed, deception, moves, skill, and a will to win.

Kevin De Bruyne is an attacking midfielder who signed with Manchester City in 2015. He had a good World Cup in 2014, scoring a decisive goal against the US in the second round. He's a very crafty, intuitive player who possesses the highly valued combination of good passing and dribbling, along with being an able goal-scorer.

KEY PLAYER STATS

	Games Played	Goals	Scoring Percentage
Jan Vertonghen	97	8	8%
Eden Hazard	80	20	25%
Kevin De Bruyne	53	12	22%

WHAT TO WATCH FOR ON TV—HOW MESSI, NEYMAR, KROOS, AND OTHERS PLAY

The Belgians are high-level passers, using accuracy, timing, rhythm, and short passing combinations about as good as any team competing in the Cup. In particular, their difference-makers (Hazard and De Bruyne) are guys who can simply outplay everyone else in one-on-one situations—crucial for setting Belgium apart from average teams.

Overall Team Rating: 8.5, pushing the gas pedal toward 9

FIFA rankings may lead one to believe Belgium is better than they actually are, based on the individual capabilities of Hazard and De Bruyne. However, as a team, they're less well-rounded than they could be.

CROATIA

A BRIEF TEAM HISTORY

For the World Cups from 1930 to 1994, Croatia was under the wing of Yugoslavia. In the 1998 World Cup, competing as Croatia, they exceeded expectations, earning third place in France. It was an amazing feat, and they were looking to duplicate it, but things slowed down on the World Cup front.

For 2002 and 2006, Croatia qualified—which is always a good thing coming out of Europe—but they advanced no farther than the group stage. They didn't qualify for 2010, but made it to Brazil 2014, only to be eliminated in the group phase.

In the process of qualifying for Russia 2018, Croatia had to navigate through a tough group of European competitors, including Iceland, Ukraine, Turkey, Finland, and Kosovo.

During the close of the 2017 European World Cup qualifications, Croatia placed second in their group, behind Iceland. This put them in a two-game playoff with Greece (who had placed second in their group, behind Belgium). The games took place on November 9 and 12, 2017. In the first game, Croatia defeated

Greece by a score of 4-1 and then tied the second game 0-0. This enabled them to qualify for the World Cup. Back in it, the Croatians are enthusiastic about their chances in Russia 2018.

FACTS ABOUT THEIR COUNTRY

Croatia's population is around 4.1 million people, with an estimated GDP of 51 billion. Like most countries, soccer is the leading sport in Croatia. Their leading goal-scorer is Davor Suker with 45 goals. Many Croatians who enjoy beer will likely be drinking Lasko, Karlovacko, and other domestic variations for the World Cup festivities and celebrations.

WHERE THE TEAM IS TODAY—TACTICS AND STRATEGIES

Croatia had a lot of promise after their good showing in the 1998 World Cup, and their hope is to stay consistent enough to live up to those expectations. Can they take the whole thing? Highly unlikely, yet anything's possible. Of the lower-ranked teams, they're definitely one that can make a big run.

Previously, Croatia has used a variety of formations, including a 4-4-2 and 3-5-2. Their challenge is to overcome being a smaller country with fewer players to choose from. They've done well with what they have, using skillful play, preferring wily ingenuity as opposed to long-ball tactics. They're certainly a team to watch out for in Russia and future World Cups.

ANTE CACIC—A BRIEF COACHING PORTRAIT

Beginning in 1986, after coaching a myriad of teams, Ante Cacic's path has led to coaching Croatia. He took the job in 2015 and has guided the team into Russia 2018. That, in itself, is a big success. Though, Croatians are wanting a bit more from their team. Still a small nation, Croatia straddles the identity of underdog meets high expectations. It's a challenging place for Coach Cacic to be, knowing they have the potential to achieve big results. Approaching each game with skillful, thoughtful soccer and not getting pushed into something else, such as forcing the ball into the box for chaotic scoring chances, would be Cacic's best approach.

KEY PLAYERS AND THEIR CHARACTERISTICS

Ivan Perisic, Mateo Kovacic, and Andrej Kramaric

Ivan Perisic, who joined Manchester United in 2017, played his first game with Croatia in 2011. Usually found on the outside, Perisic keeps defenders shaking in their boots with an explosive burst of speed, which he uses to lose slower victims with a long dribble, and even some trickery. He's a veteran who can score and set up teammates with an accurate left-foot cross—if healthy, he's a handful.

Mateo Kovacic signed with Real Madrid in 2015 after previously playing with Inter Milan. As a midfielder he's not a big scorer, but he makes up for it in the center of the field with exceptional dribbling skill which he uses to free himself up from burdensome defenders who eventually surrender to his flurry of speed and relentless ambition. Along with that, he's a feisty, relentless ball tackler, sliding in from all angles, and wheeling away from the clutch of an opponent's challenge while still halfway on the ground. A great passer, Croatia counts on his accurate distribution to guide them forward.

Andrej Kramaric, born in 1991, is a forward who made his first appearance with Croatia in 2014. He also brings valuable experience from Leicester City (2015-2016). Croatia looks forward to his goal-scoring touch for success in Russia.

KEY PLAYER STATS

	Games Played	Goals	Scoring Percentage
Ivan Perisic	62	17	27%
Mateo Kovacic	38	1	2%
Andrej Kramaric	25	7	28%

WHAT TO WATCH FOR ON TV—HOW MESSI, NEYMAR, KROOS, AND OTHERS PLAY

Croatia's a skillful team with good passing interplay, through-balls, layoffs near the top of the box, and accurate finishers. Can they duplicate past magic? That's the question. They rely on crossing, but not quite as much as others. Are they a complete team, fully equipped to take on the world? Not quite, but they have a lot of pride, which can be promising.

Overall Team Rating: 7.2, leaning toward 7

DENMARK

A BRIEF TEAM HISTORY

From 1930-1982, there was no sign of Denmark in a World Cup. In 1986, the "Dazzling Danes," as Denmark was known, led by Preben Elkjaer, Michael Laudrup, Frank Arnesen, and others, made a huge splash with big wins over Uruguay and West Germany and reached the round of 16, eventually losing to Spain.

They didn't make it to World Cups 1990 and 1994. Though, in 1998, they reached the quarterfinals, followed up by a pretty good result in 2002 as they got to the round of 16. They didn't make it to the 2006 Cup. In 2010, they were present but couldn't get out of their group. In 2014, they were unlucky—yet again—in the European qualifying process. Yet, they've maintained focus, and they're back in the big tournament, eager to make an impression at Russia 2018.

Denmark had a long haul before getting to Russia. In the European qualification games, their group included Poland, Montenegro, Romania, Armenia, and Kazakhstan. After finishing in second place behind Poland, Denmark had a two-game playoff with Ireland (who had finished second in their group behind Serbia). On November 11, 2017, they tied 0-0 in Copenhagen.

Then on November 14, 2017, Denmark soared ahead, winning 5-1 on the road in Dublin. This put the Danes in World Cup 2018.

EUROPEAN CUP

Denmark's biggest triumph as a team was winning the European Cup in 1992, defeating Germany in the final by a score of 2-0.

FACTS ABOUT THEIR COUNTRY

Denmark, the land of beautiful castles and Shakespearean tragedy, has a population of around 5.7 million people, with an estimated GDP of 302 billion. Soccer is the top sport in Denmark. The leading scorer in Denmark's history is Jon Dahl Tomasson (1997-2010), with 52 goals.

The World Cup parties will be in full swing, as many Danes will enjoy a wide selection of domestic beer, including Albani Giraf Gold and Carls Porter.

WHERE THE TEAM IS TODAY—TACTICS AND STRATEGIES

The Danes employ a firm defense, along with a thoughtful, and oftentimes patient, short-passing strategy.

Denmark has benefitted from a resurgence of talent, getting them back into the World Cup for the first time since 2010. They've had skillful teams in the past, teams with a high passing IQ, along with individual talent, but they've had a hard time bringing it all together within the hierarchy of World Cups.

They'll likely field a 3-5-2 formation. And to the best of their ability they'll encompass the quality bestowed upon them from the 1992 European champion side, as if by telepathy. But, as teams like Brazil, Argentina, and Italy know, relying on past success is a mysterious process that has a way of transposing itself across generations with no guaranteed outcome.

ÅGE HAREIDE—A BRIEF COACHING PORTRAIT

Åge Hareide accepted the Denmark coaching position in 2016. He played as a defender for his home country of Norway from 1976-1986. Don't be surprised to see a 3-5-2 formation. When they're really flowing, Coach Hareide's team has the ball moving across the field, each player getting a touch; however, the two-man game aspect—emphasized by Spain—isn't used as much as it could be for a team that is possession oriented. This may be an issue as Denmark surges forward. Another issue which will likely hold them back is their lack of star power in terms of a scoring threat. Regardless, under Hareide's direction, the team has a sophisticated approach, relying on indoor-esque skill to get scoring chances. Over the long duration of a tournament this should serve them well.

KEY PLAYERS AND THEIR CHARACTERISTICS

Simon Kjaer, Christian Eriksen, and Andreas Cornelius

The lively, energetic, passionate, heavy-handed, tattooed arms and hard tackling presence of Simon Kjaer often sends bodies flying. The center defender, born in Horsens, Denmark, who's had experience at Roma and Lille, provides a strong presence on the backline that the Danes are counting on to keep their hopes alive.

Christian Eriksen was born in 1992, the year Denmark won its only Euro Cup. As a midfielder, he's equipped with indoor skill and the ability to perform comfortably on the outside or inside. He did well with Ajax (25 goals) and signed with Tottenham in 2013. He's played with his country since 2010, and, as a consistent goal-scorer, he'll be a vital component for Danish success.

Andreas Cornelius is a head-balling racketeer of a forward with a good finishing touch around the box, accounting for his many goals. He didn't have much goal-scoring success with Cardiff City, but he's done quite well with Copenhagen. The 6′4″ Dane has played with his country since 2012 and looks to make a big impact on Russia 2018.

KEY PLAYER STATS

	Games Played	Goals	Scoring Percentage
Simon Kjaer	71	3	4%
Christian Eriksen	73	18	24%
Andreas Cornelius	15	4	26%

WHAT TO WATCH FOR ON TV—HOW MESSI, NEYMAR, KROOS, AND OTHERS PLAY

Will they be wearing white uniforms with vanilla-colored numbers on the back so that it's nearly impossible to distinguish who's who? Possibly.

Denmark's not a big goal-producing side, with the exception of Eriksen who has amassed the majority of their goals. They put together a strong team effort with the intention of patiently earning wins with finesse. At their best—dismantling a team like Liechtenstein—they're working the ball across the field, showcasing skill, getting everyone involved, and at their worst they're struggling to find answers without real star power pushing them over the top.

Overall Team Rating: 7.5

ICELAND

A BRIEF TEAM HISTORY

Way back, when zero was first used by the Sumerians and Babylonians, it was a number that represented nothing, a starting point. Today it represents the amount of times Iceland has reached the World Cup before 2018. In fact, if you were to hear that a team had no World Cup history whatsoever, you'd be talking about a number of countries, including Cambodia, Nepal, Mongolia, and Iceland. As this is Iceland's very first entry, the fans are overwhelmed with excitement.

In the European World Cup qualification games—or "Preliminary Competition," according to FIFA—Iceland did quite well, leading their group, which consisted of Croatia, Ukraine, Turkey, Finland, and Kosovo. They have a special generation of players who are ready to make history in Russia.

EUROPEAN CUP

As European Cups go, their first appearance was in 2016, where they managed to shock the world by upsetting England. Though, they eventually lost in the quarterfinals to the French hosts.

FACTS ABOUT THEIR COUNTRY

The small Atlantic island of Iceland has a population of around 330,000 people, with an estimated GDP of 21 billion. Their extremely limited population (compared with nations that have millions upon millions of citizens to choose from) makes what they're doing in modern soccer all the more intriguing. Their recent success is definitely a new experience for Icelandic soccer.

Over the years, Iceland hasn't been the biggest destination for players or coaches. For instance, in the 80s you probably wouldn't have heard Maradona say, "Barcelona has made their offer, and there's talk from Italy, and other glamorous places around the world, but what are my options like in Iceland?" In the same decade, while Platini was weighing his choices, he probably didn't say, "Arsenal, maybe. Juventus, maybe. But what about teams in Iceland? Have they called?"

Though, from time to time, some people have stopped by the small island in the North Atlantic. Fritz Buchloh—who had played goalie in Germany and also with the German national team—coached Iceland for one game in 1949.

For many years, the Icelandic government didn't allow beer consumption, but in 1989, Icelanders were allowed to drink again. Now that Iceland's a competitive World Cup contender, beer sales should rise dramatically. And celebrate they will, maybe with Einstok Arctic Pale Ale, Egils Pilsner, or Viking Sterkur.

WHERE THE TEAM IS TODAY—TACTICS AND STRATEGIES

Frankly, Iceland has been an afterthought in the world of soccer for practically all of the game's history, and they've been largely absent from almost every aspect of the sport. But despite low expectation of their success as a team, they have excelled as a talented group of underdogs.

The group they have put together is a unique combination of talent, confidence, and chemistry on the field, which is hard to teach. They have a certain "willpower" to stay in games and to win. And they hope to keep this run going for years to come.

They have a unified defense that keeps good shape in a 4-4-2 (which they'll likely stay with). Their short passing game is well orchestrated and lends them much success. As long as they keep patient with it, they should create plenty of scoring opportunities.

HEIMIR HALLGRIMSSON—A BRIEF COACHING PORTRAIT

Heimir Hallgrimsson, born in 1967, is a coach from Iceland who took on the job of coaching his country in 2013. His calm, short passing approach, emphasizing patience and confidence in the execution of passes from channel to channel, has guided Iceland to high places, including the overwhelming success at Euro 2016.

KEY PLAYERS AND THEIR CHARACTERISTICS

Kolbeinn Sigþórsson, Rúrik Gíslason, and Ragnar Sigurðsson

Kolbeinn Sigþórsson (also Sigthorsson) is a forward with experience at various clubs, including Nantes in France. Most of his club goals have come with Ajax, in the Netherlands, from 2011 to 2015. He's a veteran who first played with Iceland in 2010. A little like the Jorge Valdano of Iceland, Sigþórsson is a force up front, a bit taller, a natural scorer, a guy determined to get goals, and a good target player to have at your disposal.

Rúrik Gíslason, born in 1988, played his first game with Iceland in 2009. He's a versatile player who can play forward and midfield.

Ragnar Sigurðsson is a veteran defender who signed with Fulham in 2016. His first game with Iceland was in 2007. He's a good presence on the backline, keeping things in check while distributing the ball for his attacking teammates.

KEY PLAYER STATS

	Games Played	Goals	Scoring Percentage
Kolbeinn Sigþórsson	44	22	50%
Rúrik Gíslason	41	3	7%
Ragnar Sigurðsson	73	3	4%

WHAT TO WATCH FOR ON TV—HOW MESSI, NEYMAR, KROOS, AND OTHERS PLAY

Iceland is a very calm and confident side that does well with short passing in tight spaces. Though they have a small population and consequently fewer players too choose from, they use a pragmatic approach with good effect, challenging the idea of "bigger population equals better quality."

Overall Team Rating: 7.9, leaning toward 8.3

Iceland is a team with a knack, which is difficult to explain. Somehow, they get things done with a touch of class.

POLAND

A BRIEF TEAM HISTORY

Poland didn't play in the World Cups of 1930 and 1934. Their first attempt came in 1938, where they lost 6-5 to Brazil early in the tournament. Then, from 1950 to 1970, they weren't seen in a World Cup. Out of nowhere, during a resurgence of Polish soccer in the 1970s, they took third place in 1974. In 1978, they lost in the second round. Then, in 1982, they placed third again. In 1986, they lost in the round of 16. They went downhill after that, not qualifying for 1990, 1994, or 1998.

For 2002 and 2006, they made it back to the big tournament, but got no farther than their group. Unfortunately, they didn't qualify for 2010 and 2014. Russia 2018 represents a great opportunity for Polish soccer to get going again.

FACTS ABOUT THEIR COUNTRY

Poland, the great land between Russia and Western Europe, has a population of around 38 million people, with an estimated GDP of 508 billion.

Robert Lewandowski is one of Poland's leading scorers, along with Grzegorz (maybe we'll call him "Greg") Lato and (this is a tough one) Wlodzimierz Lubanski. Lech is a popular beer sure to be on display in bars around Poland for the World Cup.

WHERE THE TEAM IS TODAY—TACTICS AND STRATEGIES

Poland's a strong team that relies less on flash and fancy skill and more on steady pressure on both ends of the field. They work away at their opponent, trying to outlast them from the beginning of the game to the very last minute, all too willing to play deep and keep scores to a minimum.

While likely using a 4-4-2, Poland frequently pushes the ball with brisk—or forceful—passes around the field, eventually leading to a deliberate attack down the wing. Or, attempting to involve the strengths of their star player, they often initiate a strong pass to central areas around the box where Lewandowski checks to the ball, attempting to create movement off of him, but it usually results in a turnover. It's a good tactic, à la Brazilian futsal, yet, it's all fast paced and a bit rushed in its execution. Their tendency to avoid a consistent two-man game approach is partially why more errors occur. Outside of Germany, Spain, and a few others, Poland's hasty approach is a problem many countries encounter. If they were to take one possession sequence (from one side of the field to the other) and turn that into three on a consistent basis, they'd be better off.

Playing as if there are five minutes left in the game and in need of a goal to stay alive is a tactic many nations are grappling with. Poland is one of them; they're a very talented group stuck in a quagmire of expectations a few steps behind the true leaders of the game (Germany, Brazil, Argentina, and a few others).

ADAM NAWALKA—A BRIEF COACHING PORTRAIT

Adam Nawalka, born in 1957 in Poland, became head coach in 2013. Previously, he was a midfielder on the Polish national team from 1977-1980.

Under Nawalka's guidance, Poland definitely follows a "team first" approach. They're not much of individual showmen, which you'll find with Brazil. Any dribbling done will be practical in nature. In other words, no one will jump out of their seat at the sight of a flashy move. While each player is technically proficient, Coach Nawalka's direction for the team has a lot to do with getting balls into the box offensively while keeping a sound shape on the defensive line.

Offensively speaking, with Lewandowski's presence, which usually draws the attention of two defenders, other players can get open much more frequently. As the games wear on, this will only serve to Poland's advantage as Nawalka and staff intend on using Lewandowski as a playmaker as much as a goal-scorer.

KEY PLAYERS AND THEIR CHARACTERISTICS

Kamil Glik, Robert Lewandowski, and Arkadiusz Milik

Kamil Glik is a strong center defender who signed with Monaco in 2016. He plays the role of keeping things safe on the backline while initiating the attack with steady passing into the midfield and forward areas.

Robert Lewandowski, the well-known forward with Bayern Munich, has been a top player in the Bundesliga—and the world—for a few years now. His scoring touch is immaculate, while his presence in the box is always a threat. His experience and confidence give Poland a calming effect on the attacking end, which will be much needed as they pursue the trophy.

Arkadiusz Milik is a forward who signed with Napoli in 2016. He has strong scoring instincts, setting up his shot quickly with good touch around net.

KEY PLAYER STATS

	Games Played	Goals	Scoring Percentage
Kamil Glik	55	4	7%
Robert Lewandowski	91	51	56%
Arkadiusz Milik	36	12	33%

WHAT TO WATCH FOR ON TV—HOW MESSI, NEYMAR, KROOS, AND OTHERS PLAY

If anything negative is to be said about Lewandowski, it wouldn't have anything to do with his scoring talent, but more with Poland's reliance on him to score everything. Most of the attack is geared toward his success, which, in the end, might hold Poland back from truly exploring their potential. And while Lewandowski is also a good playmaker, his teammates are not quite as talented as he is on the goal-scoring front.

Overall Team Rating: 7.1

PORTUGAL

A BRIEF TEAM HISTORY

From 1930-1962, Portugal was absent from World Cups. In 1966, under the leadership and high-flying talent of Eusebio, they qualified and placed third overall—a great result for Portuguese soccer which had been quiet for so long. Then, from 1970-1982, they didn't qualify. In 1986, they lost out in the group stage. They didn't qualify, yet again, from 1990-1998.

Then a resurgence of Portuguese soccer took shape with Figo galvanizing things as they qualified for the 2002, 2006, 2010, and 2014 World Cups. Their best result in that span was 2006 when they placed fourth. That was the year Cristiano Ronaldo made his first World Cup appearance.

EUROPEAN CUP

Cristiano Ronaldo led the team—along with Nani—to the 2016 European Cup championship, the first in their nation's history.

As of 2017, Portugal placed third in the Confederations Cup held in Russia.

FACTS ABOUT THEIR COUNTRY

Portugal, a coastal country with access to the Atlantic Ocean, has a population of around 10.3 million people, with an estimated GDP of 213 billion.

At the 2006 World Cup, Portugal was given FIFA's "Most Entertaining Team Award." There are many Portuguese beers available around World Cup time, including Super Bock, Coral, and Sagres.

WHERE THE TEAM IS TODAY—TACTICS AND STRATEGIES

After winning the 2016 European Cup, Portugal is riding high with celebratory emotion. Many saw the final game between France and Portugal as a mismatch of talent (France) and luck (Portugal). In their defense, the match was played in France with the odds heavily against Portugal. If anything, the Portuguese played a good game, considering. But, the overall performance of Portugal in Euro 2016 falls in line with the underlining theme of their performances since about 2006: They're a middle-of-the-road program, albeit one that resides in the upper echelon of the middle, which relies too heavily on one player—Ronaldo.

Under the leadership of Pepe, they have plenty of experienced defenders that are good, but not great. Short passing they have, along with a dynamic counterattack administered by players that possess good technique, but, without their star, in the event Ronaldo gets injured or acquires multiple yellow cards, they're a wavering team, looking for that extra push. They'll likely field a 4-4-2 with a heavy emphasis on getting Ronaldo the ball out wide.

FERNANDO SANTOS—A BRIEF COACHING PORTRAIT

Fernando Santos, born in 1954, is a former defender who played professionally with Portuguese clubs Estoril and Maritimo from 1973 to 1987. He coached Greece from 2010 to 2014 and then took on the Portuguese job in 2014.

Sometimes coaches get lucky and find themselves with unbelievable talent…players so good that, at times, the coach questions whether they should even show up at all. Santos' approach with Portugal involves strong defense, aligned with spirited wing play, utilizing the salient talents of Ronaldo and Nani.

KEY PLAYERS AND THEIR CHARACTERISTICS

Cristiano Ronaldo and Nani

Cristiano Ronaldo, listed by Forbes in 2017 as the highest paid soccer player in the world,[6] is a forward with Real Madrid, where he's received much of his current attention. Prior to that, he emerged as a star player with Manchester United, teamed with Rooney, Giggs, Scholes, and others. He's a prolific goal-scorer who used to rely on pure speed—and astonishing trickery—to dazzle his way around defenders. But nowadays his dribbling has slowed down a tad, and he often looks to use his impressive leaping ability—featured on *Tested to the Limit* presented by Castrol Edge*—to soar above defenders for aerial goals.

Nani is a talented attacking player usually found on the outside. He uses bursts of speed along with aggressive north-and-south dribbling to get downfield. He's a proficient scorer and a great setup man.

KEY PLAYER STATS

	Games Played	Goals	Scoring Percentage
Cristiano Ronaldo	147	79	53%
Nani	112	24	21%

WHAT TO WATCH FOR ON TV—HOW MESSI, NEYMAR, KROOS, AND OTHERS PLAY

Even though Ronaldo and Nani have slowed down a bit, they're still integral pieces to the team's positive momentum. Portugal relies on steady possession with quick one-two punches from their star attacking players, who, in their younger days, were teammates on Manchester United. Portugal tends to play a lot of balls in the air to Ronaldo, a good jumper, who has plenty of success with crosses.

Overall Team Rating: 8

---

* A video from 2011 which used sports science to test Cristiano Ronaldo's athletic abilities.

SERBIA

A BRIEF TEAM HISTORY

Serbia's first World Cup as Serbia was in 2010. (Prior to 2010, they competed in World Cups as Serbia and Montenegro and Yugoslavia.) In 2010, as Serbia (without the Montenegro), they made it to South Africa but didn't get out of their group. Serbia did not make it to Brazil in 2014. A brief World Cup experience, indeed, but one they hope to improve upon in Russia 2018 and down the road.

FACTS ABOUT THEIR COUNTRY

Serbia's population is around 7 million people, with a GDP of about 42 billion. Many Serbians will likely have Jelen Pivo beer at their disposal during World Cup games.

WHERE THE TEAM IS TODAY—TACTICS AND STRATEGIES

Serbia will likely go with a 4-4-2 formation. To win the World Cup outright will take a substantial effort from Serbia, one that might require the equivalent of 36 saves from the Serbian goalie in each game. As a newer nation to the world of soccer, and one with less experience at that, Serbia is looking to build on successful outings as they enter the next phase of their international soccer agenda. From years under the umbrella of Yugoslavia, which provided a formidable program, they have a good place to start.

SLAVOLJUB MUSLIN—A BRIEF COACHING PORTRAIT

Slavoljub Muslin was born in Yugoslavia and began coaching Serbia in 2016. Prior to this job, he coached a score of teams, which included some French clubs. His approach with this team has been to keep the passing combination play intact so that Tadic and Mitrovic can exude their talent up front.

KEY PLAYERS AND THEIR CHARACTERISTICS

Aleksandar Mitrovic, Zoran Tosic, and Dusan Tadic

Aleksandar Mitrovic is a good target forward who positions well and can finish around goal. He signed with Newcastle United in 2015, as they recognized his scoring touch. Since his first game with Serbia in 2013, he's been a pretty consistent goal-scorer, and Serbians are hoping for this trend to continue in Russia.

Zoran Tosic is a veteran and able scorer who signed with CSKA Moscow in 2010 and has played with Serbia since 2007. He plays on the outside and possesses good dribbling skills in small spaces with the ability to maneuver across the top of the box to create scoring chances.

Dusan Tadic, born in Yugoslavia, is an elusive midfielder who joined Southampton in 2014. His all-around talent has served him well in the EPL. He's also a steady goal-scoring option for Serbia with a good shot from outside. Not only that, he's the playmaker; whether it's dribbling past opponents or delivering a clever back-heel, Serbia has a better chance to win with Tadic delivering the ball.

KEY PLAYER STATS

	Games Played	Goals	Scoring Percentage
Aleksander Mitrovic	32	10	31%
Zoran Tosic	76	11	14%
Dusan Tadic	48	12	25%

WHAT TO WATCH FOR ON TV—HOW MESSI, NEYMAR, KROOS, AND OTHERS PLAY

Midfield interplay and active movement toward goal will define Serbia's chances to win. The combination of Tadic and Mitrovic is vital for any possible success. They have linked up numerous times in the past, and their chemistry should be on full display. Whether the defense can avoid sloppy errors on the backline is another story. Should they correct tiny issues here and there, Serbia will be a team to reckon with this World Cup and those to come.

Overall Team Rating: 6.5, leaning toward 7

SWEDEN

A BRIEF TEAM HISTORY

Sweden has one of the more curious World Cup records around. In the early days, they did quite well, then sort of fizzled out. In the 1930 World Cup, they didn't compete. In 1934, they made the quarterfinals. For the 1938 World Cup, they placed fourth.

Then, in 1950, they placed third. Things were looking good for old Sweden. However, for 1954, they didn't qualify. As hosts in 1958, they earned second place. Back at it! So far, so good. However, at this juncture, things began to go downhill.

They didn't qualify in 1962 or 1966. In 1970, they didn't get out of their group. In 1974, they got to the second round only. At Argentina in 1978, they didn't get out of their group. Things got worse in 1982 and 1986, as they didn't qualify. In 1990, they were back, but couldn't get out of their group. Then, in 1994, they did very well, earning third place. But, for France in 1998, they didn't qualify. Back at it in 2002 and 2006, they made the big tournament but were eliminated in the round of 16. And, similar to their track record of being consistently inconsistent, they didn't qualify for 2010 or 2014.

During European World Cup qualifications, Sweden finished second in their group behind France. As a result, they went into a two-game playoff with Italy (who had finished second in their group behind Spain). And so it was, for the first time in a long time (1958, to be exact), Italy would not be going to the World Cup. In the opening game, Sweden won 1-0 on November 10, 2017, in Sweden. Then, a few days later, on November 13, 2017, a 0-0 tie held in Milan, Italy, sent Sweden to the 2018 World Cup.

Outside of the World Cup, Sweden has won the Nordic Football Championship (1924-2001) nine times. They also won the gold medal in the 1948 Olympics.

FACTS ABOUT THEIR COUNTRY

Welcome to Sweden—the land of King Carl XVI Gustaf, Volvo, Ikea, and other great products. Sweden's population is around 10 million people, with an estimated GDP of 517 billion.

Sweden's all-time leading scorer is Zlatan Ibrahimović, with 62 goals. In second place is good old Sven Rydell (1923-1932), with 49. Pripps Bla is a popular Swedish beer (dating back to 1828) sure to make the rounds as people watch their team on television.

WHERE THE TEAM IS TODAY—TACTICS AND STRATEGIES

Sweden hasn't found the great results that teams of yore had. Though, with a resurgence of Swedish soccer on the national scene (since the 1990s) and the implementation of Ibrahimović in recent years, they've gained momentum. Essentially, within the forest of European talent, they're a middle-of-the-road team trying to find their form.

With this team, at this point in history, their chances of winning the World Cup in Russia are close to zero. In fact, to win the whole thing, to walk away with the coveted World Cup trophy, they'll need a mythical effort, something on the order of 72 small miracles in each game. It would be pretty impressive if they even made the second round. Making it out of their group will likely involve three consecutive ties, hoping for the same from their opponents and praying that points go in their favor. The odd thing about Sweden is that they're not terrible, by any stretch of the imagination. But, in the post-Ibrahimović era, aside from qualifying *for* the World Cup, which is an impressive achievement in and of itself, things don't look incredibly optimistic for Sweden *at* the World Cup.

On the positive side, they do have a group of experienced players that can keep games close and pull out victories here and there. Will it be enough to get into the semifinals and possibly win the whole thing? It's unlikely, but that's the beauty of sports.

They'll probably take up a 4-4-2 formation, a reliable option. They don't play the two-man game very often; if they do it's out of necessity rather than a strategic means to improve chemistry. And they prefer attacking down the flanks.

Essentially, they're a group of serviceable players, trying to find a magical formula, which may not be there. But, on the big stage, with a little push, things can often come together in the right way, and that's what Sweden is counting on.

JANNE ANDERSSON—A BRIEF COACHING PORTRAIT

Janne Andersson was born in 1962 in Sweden and took over coaching the team in 2016. His quest is to build on the passing combinations they'll need in order to stay consistent against better competition; without fancy dribblers, this will be of great importance. Also for Andersson, sustaining the willpower of the team is of paramount concern, as Sweden tries to pull past better teams.

KEY PLAYERS AND THEIR CHARACTERISTICS

Mikael Lustig, Sebastian Larsson, and Marcus Berg

Mikael Lustig is an active defender who has played with Sweden since 2008. He brings the experience needed to help guide his team past the recent lulls of the Swedish World Cup experience.

Sebastian Larsson is a versatile midfielder who joined Sunderland in 2011 and has played with Sweden since 2008. Whether it's a curling shot from a free kick or a lower driven ball guided into the corner of the net, Larsson's goal-scoring experience—which has consistently been on display during his club performances—is vital for Sweden to move forward in the tournament. On top of that, as a veteran, his management of the game—with vision and passing—is a crucial element to Sweden's success.

Marcus Berg is a forward who first played for Sweden in 2008. He's a reliable goal-scorer, very good at tapping—or guiding—in crosses, but can finish from most areas around the box. Now in his early 30s, should he stay healthy, he's a focal point for Sweden's attack.

KEY PLAYER STATS

	Games Played	Goals	Scoring Percentage
Mikael Lustig	62	6	9%
Sebastian Larsson	94	6	6%
Marcus Berg	51	18	35%

WHAT TO WATCH FOR ON TV—HOW MESSI, NEYMAR, KROOS, AND OTHERS PLAY

Sweden often relies on attacking the flanks to try and get accurate service into the box. Can they get goals other ways? Yes. But this is typically their main approach. And this may be one of the things holding them back. Another will be a lack of star power and creative ingenuity. Though, with a strong effort, they have the capacity to overcome these barriers.

Overall Team Rating: 7

SWITZERLAND

A BRIEF TEAM HISTORY

Switzerland, the on-again, off-again central-European, middle-of-the-road program, often slightly better than other middle-of-the-road teams, had early success with the World Cup, relatively speaking, and then ran out of steam.

Switzerland didn't compete in World Cup 1930, the first grand extravaganza in Uruguay, but made it to the quarterfinals in 1934 and 1938. Their string of average began in 1950, when they fizzled out in the group phase. World Cup 1954, which was held in Switzerland, was better, as they made the quarterfinals. Though, for Sweden in 1958, they didn't compete.

Things got a little better—but not so much—in 1962 and 1966, as they made the tournaments but got no farther than the group phase. Nothing more than a dalliance before twenty years of silence. As things played out, from 1970 to 1990, they didn't qualify. A long time for Switzerland to be out of World Cup action.

But, in 1994, on their epic comeback, they got to the round of 16, a big success, considering. However, in 1998 and 2002, they didn't even qualify. In true Swiss form, they mounted a comeback, and, by 2006, they were back and made it to the round of 16. Unfortunately, they lost in penalty kicks to the Ukraine. In 2010, they weren't so lucky and were unable to escape Group H, which consisted of Spain, Chile, and Honduras. And, for 2014, they got back on track, eventually losing 1-0 in the round of 16 to Argentina, thanks to a goal from Di Maria.

In the closing months of 2017, during European World Cup qualifications, Switzerland finished second in their group behind Portugal. This led to a two-game playoff with Northern Ireland (who finished second in their group behind Germany). The games were played on November 9 and 12, 2017. Switzerland won an aggregate victory of 1-0, guaranteeing a place in Russia 2018.

FACTS ABOUT THEIR COUNTRY

Switzerland, a beautiful tourist destination, has a population of about 8.4 million people, with an estimated GDP of 651 billion.

Josef Hugi is Switzerland's top World Cup goal-scorer, with five or six in 1954. (One Wikipedia page indicates five goals,[7] and another indicates six.[8] At FIFA's website the tally is six goals.[9] Short of conducting a full-on investigation, which would include exhaustive overseas calls to the Swiss Football Association, it would appear he is Switzerland's leader with five or six goals; probably six.)

Glasses of Erdinger or Vollmond beer will likely make the rounds as Swiss fans watch their team from home soil.

WHERE THE TEAM IS TODAY—TACTICS AND STRATEGIES

Switzerland is a team in the mix—on the lower end of very good, or, one might say they're in the upper part of the middle pack. They're not a great world power—and likely never will be—but they're a competitive team looking to get their program in a steady stream of consistent success at World Cup level. And, like all teams at their level, they have the potential to pull off a miraculous World Cup championship run.

They're not a classical long-ball team, nor are they short-passing experts; however, they're comfortable in a half-field possession game and known to use a 4-3-3 or a 4-2-3-1 formation. Regardless, they lie somewhere in between, slugging it out with strong team cohesion, minus true star power.

Essentially, as one of the teams of the upper-middle pack least likely to reach the semifinals, they're a strong sparring partner for the world's elite, with the ability to defeat any team on any given day (with a little luck, of course).

VLADIMIR PETKOVIC—A BRIEF COACHING PORTRAIT

Vladimir Petkovic was born in Yugoslavia and spent his playing career with various club teams from Bosnia, Slovenia, and Switzerland, where he played as a midfielder from 1981-1999. He also coached a variety of teams for short intervals, and before taking the Swiss national team job in 2014, he was coach of Lazio in Italy.

He's using the talent he has, combining consistent defensive play to make a run at teams with a mix of short passing and fundamental attacks down the flanks to create scoring opportunities. Without dominating star players, it's a difficult task for any coach to oversee.

KEY PLAYERS AND THEIR CHARACTERISTICS

Stephan Lichtsteiner, Granit Xhaka, and Josip Drmic

Stephan Lichtsteiner, a defender who plays with Juventus, is a steady player on the flank that brings leadership and experience.

Granit Xhaka is a strong tackler who favors his left foot as a means to distribute the ball downfield to teammates.

Josip Drmic is a skilled forward with experience from playing on a handful of German clubs who can make his teammates look good with a perfect pass or get a goal for himself with great touch around net.

KEY PLAYER STATS

	Games Played	Goals	Scoring Percentage
Stephan Lichtsteiner	93	8	8%
Granit Xhaka	55	8	14%
Josip Drmic	26	9	34%

WHAT TO WATCH FOR ON TV—HOW MESSI, NEYMAR, KROOS, AND OTHERS PLAY

Switzerland has a talented group intent on getting their team—and country—out of the quagmire of average performances in the modern World Cup era. They have a lot of skill and players that can make a difference, which, if combined in the right way, with a bit of momentum, can turn out to serve them well on this endeavor and even four years down the road in 2022, as they're a program that is planning for future success.

On the field of play, despite having credible, skillful players who have loads of European club experience, the Swiss suffer from the "fizzle-out syndrome," which others, like Ireland, Greece, and Turkey (who coincidentally didn't make the World Cup), also suffer from. Meaning, they do very well up to a point, then, they abandon what got them there, and their hard work predictably falls to shambles. Whether it's a string of good passes or general momentum, something falls apart; someone gets aggressive with a pass or simply turns the ball over.

One might successfully argue that without star players, it will be hard—if not impossible—for the Swiss eleven to overcome the challenges before them. Though, from the Swiss perspective, coming together as one group, while staying consistent, might be the best option. And, based on their experience within the high-tier quality of European competition, anything is possible.

Overall Team Rating: 7

SOUTH AMERICA (4 ½)

Brazil, Argentina, Uruguay, Peru, Colombia

BRAZIL

A BRIEF TEAM HISTORY

World Cup titles: 5 (1958, 1962, 1970, 1994, 2002)

The amazing, tantalizing, and always primetime Brazilians have a long and interesting history with the greatest game around. Before Brazil became the bellwether of world soccer, they didn't start out so great.

Before 1950, Argentina and Uruguay were the leaders in South America. No samba, yet. In the 1930 World Cup, Brazil lost out in the group phase. In 1934, which was conceived as a straight-elimination competition, Brazil lost their first game to Spain. By 1938, Brazil improved, getting to the semifinals and eventually placing third overall.

Brazil came so close in the 1950 final, held in the Maracana Stadium with some 200,000 spectators. Uruguay scored the final goal in what turned out to be a 2-1 victory for them, and silence crept through the stadium. As Pele has famously said, his father cried over the result, and Pele promised him a championship for Brazil. In 1954, Brazil lost to Hungary in the quarterfinals, despite goals from Djalma Santos and Julinho.

The big year came in 1958 as Pele and Garrincha—with help from players like Zagallo and Vava—thrilled the crowds with exciting, skillful play, establishing a new era in world soccer. The 17-year-old Pele helped lead Brazil to their first World Cup title against the hosts Sweden in the final. Pele would represent every aspect of a complete offensive player.[10] With Pele and Garrincha arriving around the same time, it was just the beginning of an unbelievable run for Brazil that would span decades as they redefined style, shaping the game with their own unique approach on the field.

Right away, in 1962, they repeated as champions in Chile. Pele resigned to the bench early due to injury. From there, Garrincha took over with one of the elite individual performances in tournament history, scoring multiple goals and impressing the world audience with his uncanny ability to dribble with quickness, patience, and complete authority.

By 1966, Brazil was outmuscled by "Europe." There was a feeling from Brazil that the Europeans outmanned them, which was evident with forceful fouls. The rough play got to them, and they regrouped for 1970, adding some punch to their spirit.

Arguably one of the best teams in history, the 1970 Brazilian side flourished with salient performances from Pele, Tostao, Jairzinho, and Rivelino backed by elegant defending from Brito, Piazza, Carlos Alberto, and Clodoaldo—defenders who complemented the offensive talent up front with skill of their own. The championship run was their third title. Brazil would place fourth in 1974 and then third in 1978.

With Zico and other dazzling players, Brazil moved on from the 70s and into 1982, showcasing the Brazilian flair for soccer as an art under coach Tele Santana. He was a coach that wanted his players to be showmen. Falcao, Zico, Eder, Socrates, and Junior played the game the way many Brazilians thought it should remain: as an artistic display of integrity. Unluckily, they lost in a thriller to Italy, the eventual champions.

By 1986, with Socrates and Junior as veteran leaders, they added some speed with Careca and Muller. Unlucky again, they lost in penalty kicks in an epic showdown with France in the quarterfinals.

In 1990, they added Dunga as a defensive midfielder with Valdo in the attack, joining Careca and Muller. It was a quick, dynamic team with an energetic approach. They had all the skill and firepower of Brazilian teams from the past but with a little more speed. In group play, they defeated Sweden, Costa Rica, and Scotland. Still, expectations again fell short as they were outdone in the second round thanks to a flash of brilliance from Maradona to Caniggia for the winning goal.

In 1994, with a new duo up front consisting of Bebeto and Romario, Brazil was twenty-four years without the championship trophy they wanted so much. In a turn of events, under coach Carlos Alberto Parreira, they were arguably playing more defensively than in the past. In fact, the Brazilian public was upset with the style put forth, regarding their first-place finish as something to be expected, yet a feat that could've been more glamorous had the team displayed more of the *futebol arte,* or *joga bonito.* Imagine that: They won the biggest tournament on earth, and the public wasn't satisfied, essentially saying, "Not good enough." They wanted more style, more finesse, more offensive electricity. They wanted what every team theoretically strives for in a game: a winning team with class.

The 1998 World Cup was another great result on paper (for most nations, anyway), but a bitter disappointment for Brazilians, as they lost to France in the final. Brazil would come back in 2002 with a multitalented attack led by Rivaldo, Ronaldo, and Ronaldinho. There was something unfair about that team. It was as if they said, "If you thought 1998 had next to unstoppable offensive power, we still have Denilson coming off the bench, and now we're introducing a guy named Ronaldinho. Who's he? Eh, no one, really. Just a new player. He's okay. We'll see." How could opponents compete with that? It was a high-octane attack similar to the 1970 side in that it was one of the best offensive combinations of players from any era. It was the first World Cup held in Asia, and Brazil won in style, defeating Germany 2-0 in the final.

The 2006 World Cup in Germany wouldn't be so kind to Brazil, as they lost in the second round to France. Again, in 2010, with a team led by Kaka and Robinho, Brazil would find disappointment, losing to the Netherlands in the elimination stage.

By 2014, with Neymar leading the charge, Brazil was ready to make a comeback; it came with mounting pressure as they played host. Unfortunately, with a lineup that didn't strike anyone as very Brazilian, they would lose a crushing—and shocking—defeat to Germany in the semifinals by a score of 7-1. Yikes.

OLYMPIC GOLD

Brazil would make up for the 2014 World Cup—somewhat, anyway—two years later in the Olympics. Oddly enough, with all

Brazil's success in world soccer, the Olympics had always been out of reach. Brazil happened to be the hosts, and, low and behold, they met Germany in the gold medal match. For the Olympics, the rules were a little different, only allowing a handful of players above the age of 23. Yet, it was still "Brazil vs. Germany" with a chance for redemption. The stakes couldn't have been higher for Brazil. Throughout the games, practically every conversation in Portuguese was about the Brazilian soccer team; it seemed as if every other event was politely discarded. The Brazilians wanted that gold in soccer. In a great back-and-forth game, both sides were playing at the highest level. Led by Neymar, Brazil took it to them, winning their first gold medal for men's soccer.

With this achievement, Brazil finally added the Olympics to their list of accomplishments, including the World Cup and South American championships.

SOUTH AMERICAN COMPETITIONS

Brazil has won the Copa America* eight times in 1919, 1922, 1949, 1989, 1997, 1999, 2004, and 2007.

FACTS ABOUT THEIR COUNTRY

Brazil, the land of soccer, is a very interesting place. It's a large country, geographically and population-wise, with over 206

---

* The South American Championship (also known as the South American Football Championship) began in 1916. It was called the Copa America in 1975.

million people, and a GDP of about 1.5 trillion. The largest city is Sao Paulo with an estimated population of 12 million.

Historically, Brazil has evidence of human activity likely dating back 11,000 years, as well as pottery found from around 6,000 BC. The Portuguese first established their presence in Brazil back in 1500 AD, only eight years after Christopher Columbus made his voyage across the Atlantic.

The Lost City of Z, a book written by David Grann, explores the journey of Colonel Fawcett, a British explorer in the early 20th Century, who was mapping the area of Bolivia, Peru, and western Brazil, while also searching for a mythical lost city filled with gold.

In today's Brazil, many soccer players search for their own chest of "gold" by way of professional contracts. Brazilian players are highly favored around the world. Cafu is the Brazilian leader in caps, with 142. Pele is the leading scorer, with 77. Pele also has three World Cup titles to his name: 1958, 1962, and 1970.

Brazil is known for great food, including steaks and exotic pizza varieties. As World Cup Russia progresses, many people watching on TV will likely enjoy domestic beer, including Eisenbahn.

WHERE THE TEAM IS TODAY—TACTICS AND STRATEGIES

Brazil may have come up empty handed in the 2016 Copa America, but their defense throughout the 2018 World Cup qualification games has been strong, rooted in quick double teams and active individual talent.

Brazil has built their exciting attack around the fleet feet of Neymar, along with a group that exudes the classic Brazilian flair mixed with a sound passing structure that can be found in Europe. With this offensive group of young players in place, Brazil is looking to capitalize on a creative pulse which has been lacking in the past two World Cups. (See appendix under Brazil, "Brazil Looking for World Cup Magic Again," for bonus material.)

Brazil will probably go with a 4-3-3. As usual, they'll be a favorite, and, depending who you ask, they always have the potential to win the whole thing.

TITE—A BRIEF COACHING PORTRAIT

Brazil will be coached by Tite for World Cup Russia. How did Tite end up in this esteemed position with a chance to win an unprecedented sixth title for Brazil? As a player, his career as a midfielder with a handful of Brazilian clubs spanned from 1978-1989. As coach, he's been in charge of a wide assortment of teams, including Gremio and Corinthians.

He has every intention of keeping the momentum from the 2016 Olympics going forward in a positive direction, with the flashy style of the past in place along with a strict policy of defense and team organization. Tite guided the team through qualifications with relative ease, and the whole world will be curious to see if he can repeat the process in Russia.

KEY PLAYERS AND THEIR CHARACTERISTICS

Neymar, Coutinho, and Willian

If video games translate to real-life soccer, the Danish wiz, Mohamad Al-Bacha, who is the FIFA Interactive World Cup 2017 champion, says Neymar is one of his top five because he is one of the most powerful[11] players to use in electronic land. Outside of video games, Neymar—who has played with Santos, Barcelona, and Paris Saint-Germain—has turned into one of the game's biggest names due to his flashy skill, dribbling ability, tricks, and an eye for goal. With Neymar, who is equipped with a skinny frame and legs no bigger than Matthias Sindelar's, you'll see a lot of artful play as he displays a unique touch on the ball combined with a keen sense of finding teammates with decisive passes in a crowd or creating a scoring chance with a give and go. Around the corner of the box is where defenders have reason for concern. He's quick, fast, and fearless going forward, willing to take hits along the way like a running back in the NFL, thus creating many set piece opportunities. Few players display a knack for dribbling in small spaces and also big swooping runs down the line—à la Kaka in his prime—but Neymar's one of them, showing off his big dribble ability against Paraguay in a 2017 qualifier with a goal that started some twenty yards behind his own half line, resulting in a subtle finish. (See appendix under Brazil, "Neymar Living Up to Pele," for bonus material.)

Couthinho provides a spark with a strong shot and the ability to finish around the box. He's proving to be a valuable asset for Brazil, and knowing as much, Liverpool got their hands on him in 2013.

Willian is a player who often ends up being the most valuable performer on the field. He is very quick and is able to dribble past opponents with relative ease. The Chelsea man is a player to keep an eye on as he provides explosive offense that creates openings, often around the wing, for him and his teammates to exploit.

KEY PLAYER STATS

	Games Played	Goals	Scoring Percentage
Neymar	83	53	63%
Couthinho	32	8	25%
Willian	53	8	15%

WHAT TO WATCH FOR ON TV—HOW MESSI, NEYMAR, KROOS, AND OTHERS PLAY

Based on Rivaldo's notorious flop near the corner flag in the 2002 World Cup, Brazil might forever be worthy of the "Top Flop Team" award...an honor Neymar's team may want to stray away from.

Over the years, every team in the world has been inspired by Brazil. Interestingly, in today's game, Brazil is now caught in a position of keeping up with the pack, as one of the gods of world soccer. Since 2008, Spain and Germany have continued on a path of success in the modern era (even though Spain is likely returning to a path of normal). Now, somewhat lost by comparison, Brazil has to learn from these teams in an attempt to use tactics from the "new" refined European style (which relies on principles of sound possession to outwill an opponent), while redefining their "old" samba rhythm.

If Neymar and supporting staff are healthy, Brazil should have a huge impact on the tournament. Watch for quick, upbeat passing, with Neymar seeing plenty of the ball, exuding his dribbling prowess whenever he can, exploiting the sides while also turning into the middle, causing danger for opposing defenders. With Brazil, quick combination passes open up the wings for overlapping outside defenders who are chosen for their ability to attack down the line. If all these parts are operating at full-throttle, Brazil should be a handful for any opponent and a pleasure to watch.

Overall Team Rating: 9.2, bordering on 8.8

Despite Neymar and the successful World Cup qualification run making it appear as though Brazil is a solid 10, the samba beat struggled in the 2016 Copa America, and many lineup choices are not reflective of Brazil's true artistic potential. For that reason, even though they're a favorite to win the whole thing, they are a 9.2, slipping into the 8.8 range.

ARGENTINA

A BRIEF TEAM HISTORY

World Cup titles: 2 (1978, 1986)

The Argentineans got off to a good start in their World Cup endeavors, placing second at the first ever tournament held in Uruguay in 1930. Goals from Carlos Peucelle and Guillermo Stabile were not enough to defeat the hosts, Uruguay, as Argentina lost in the final by a score of 4-2. Then things took an interesting turn for the worse.

Argentina lost early in 1934 and subsequently didn't participate in 1938, 1950, *or* 1954. They braced for 1958 with more optimism; however, they finished dead last in their group, and left Sweden feeling utterly disappointed.

Things weren't much better in Chile in 1962, as Argentina finished third in their group. Yet another early elimination for the team that had placed second in the very first World Cup.

Things would get better in 1966, as they finished second in their group behind West Germany. Yet, they lost in the quarterfinals to the hosts, and eventual champs, England, by a score of 1-0 in

Wembley Stadium in front of over 90,000 people with a strong bias for the home team.

By 1970, it was back to the old story of not qualifying. In 1974, they had another idea, placing second in their group behind Poland. However, they lost in their second-round group, finishing last behind East Germany.

During these years, win or lose, Argentina fielded teams that showcased players that were individually a little better than others, such as Onega from the 1960s. They may not have been doing well in World Cups, but they had a certain craft about their touch with a little swagger to the way they dribbled—a hint of things to come. They were the type of players that, right away, caught your eye. But considering their somewhat unstable on-again, off-again relationship with the World Cup, there was something holding them back.

As hosts, 1978 would be Argentina's year. They started things out by finishing second in their group behind Italy. In the second round, things were broken up into Groups A and B. There were concerns, particularly from Brazilian constituents, that Argentina—who, at the time, was under a strict dictatorship—rigged the all-important match with Peru. Some assert the referees were manipulated; others claim the Peruvian players were approached with bribes and threats beforehand; while still others insist both the referees *and* Peruvian players were instructed to give the game over to the hosts. The game ended in a 6-0 victory for Argentina as Kempes led the charge with two. Within the group, Argentina tied Brazil. Based on points and goal differential, Argentina advanced to the championship while Brazil was forced to play for the consolation. So when Argentina defeated the Netherlands for the final, many speculated it wasn't the fairest of tournaments.

Making it to the second round in 1982, Argentina was quickly eliminated in Group C with defeats from superpowers Italy and Brazil. Argentina's new star, Diego Maradona (who nearly made the 1978 squad), would have to wait four more years for his shot at glory.

By 1986, led by arguably the greatest player of all time, Maradona, Argentina had to their advantage *a new era of refereeing*. FIFA had listened to the calls for change at the last World Cup. There were many complaints about the game getting out of control with unnecessary rough play, leaving creative types like Maradona on the ground more often than they'd like to be. Thanks to many factors, including a well-rounded Argentinean side, along with the brilliance of Maradona and the hand of Maradona, Argentina would win the championship in stylish form, making it their second title. In 1990, Argentina, led by Maradona, received the runner-up award, losing to West Germany.

Over the course of 16 years, the tournaments of 1994, 1998, 2002, 2006, and 2010 featured various talented players for their respective time, including Zanetti, Ortega, Veron, Crespo, Tevez, Riquelme, and Messi, and each was a decent showing for the two-time champs, yet Argentina failed to lift the trophy.

In 1994, they lost in the second round to Romania. In 1998, they lost in the quarterfinals to the Netherlands. The 2002 World Cup wasn't very good for Argentina as they failed to get out of their group. At Germany in 2006, they lost to Germany in the quarterfinals. Yet again in South Africa in 2010, they lost to Germany in the quarterfinals.

In 2014, led by Messi and a talented group of players fit for a championship, Argentina made the finals, with a good showing against Germany, but it wasn't enough. As for Russia 2018, seeing that it could likely be Messi's last, the people of Argentina are looking forward to a third championship.

SOUTH AMERICAN COMPETITIONS

Argentina has won the Copa America 14 times in 1921, 1925, 1927, 1929, 1937, 1941, 1945, 1946, 1947, 1955, 1957, 1959, 1991, and 1993.

FACTS ABOUT THEIR COUNTRY

Argentina has an estimated population of 43 million people, with a GDP of about 541 billion. Without a doubt, soccer is the number one sport in Argentina and has been for some time.

Argentina's captain during their 1978 World Cup championship run was Daniel Passarella. Messi won the Adidas Golden Ball* (i.e., the MVP) at the 2014 World Cup.

Of the many beers Argentineans can choose from, Antares will likely be one floating around during World Cup matches. Also, Santiago Auld, from the bar Palermo Groove located in beautiful

---

* Members of FIFA, known as the "FIFA Technical Study Group," determined the winner.

Buenos Aires, pointed out that Quilmes was a popular beer from 2014, adding, "On the finals owners and public fans get wasted before [the] end of [the] match!"* Santiago, like many Argentineans, is picking his country to win the 2018 World Cup, because, as he said, "we have Messi."

WHERE THE TEAM IS TODAY—TACTICS AND STRATEGIES

With the ability to stifle opponents defensively by putting high pressure on the ball, the Argentineans are always a difficult team to play against.

Offensively, they can push the pace of the game quickly with crisp passes, dizzying their opponents with possession. They tend to cross the ball less (than say, Ireland); rather, they attack with intelligent passes combined with elite skill. Most players on the field at any given time are playmakers eager to make a difference in the game.

If having a temper is a strategy, they use it effectively at times, while other times it turns into their own worst enemy. If they get down a goal, and things aren't going their way, it usually takes one guy—say, Mascherano—to throw a temper tantrum,† berating the referee (sometimes multiple referees), and the rest will follow.

Argentina will probably go with a 4-4-2 (however, they've previously used different variations). Though, from time to time,

---

* Santiago kindly provided information by email.

† Which varies in severity, depending, of course, on the circumstances.

strategy is thrown out the window, and they rely, instead, on good old-fashioned soccer know-how—an elegant "tactic" they were accused of in 2010 under the guidance of Maradona.

Whether no strategy is a strategy or whether any such accusation is true, over time, Argentina has effectively gained two World Cups and a myriad of South American championships. As good as they are, with talent from wing to wing, this team's approach, with a sound footing in soccer know-how, should be no different.

EDGARDO BAUZA—A BRIEF COACHING PORTRAIT

Edgardo Bauza played as a defender from 1977 to 1991 in Argentina, Colombia, and Mexico. He then coached a variety of teams before taking over Argentina in 2016. Under Coach Bauza, Argentina brings a strong defense with aggressive tacklers and a pressing, relentless attack geared around Messi.

Though, as past performances have illustrated, constantly putting the ball at Messi's feet, with the idea of carrying a nation, could be holding his talent back, keeping his team at bay. When he's constantly getting the ball, with expectations of something magical looming in the air, it might just be a detriment to the team's fluidity.

The best Argentinean attack could be to get the rest of the team to be the stars, allowing them the majority of possession (i.e., as many touches as possible). As with Barcelona, wherein all players are constantly touching the ball and Messi is benefitting from their masterful possession interplay, it might be in Argentina's best interest to copy this approach (the best they can). After all, when a championship is on the line, a free-flowing, goal-hungry Argentina is a little different from a highly structured Barcelona.

All these matters should be on the mind of Coach Bauza as he tries to implement the best course of action for his super-talented team, a group that struggled a bit in qualifications.

KEY PLAYERS AND THEIR CHARACTERISTICS

Lionel Messi, Gonzalo Higuain, Angel Di Maria, Ezequiel Lavezzi, and Javier Mascherano

Lionel Messi—who has won the award for best player in the world in 2009, 2010, 2011, 2012, and 2015—is regarded by many as the best player of all time. Any discussion about such a thing really comes down to facts on paper and opinion. For those who believe facts on paper rule such arguments, then Pele would be the obvious choice, with three World Cup titles under his belt. Maradona—who shook the world with his amazing abilities—would be next, with one title to his credit. The fantastic Garrincha comes to mind, with two titles. Then Messi—Argentina's answer to Maradona—is found in the same company as great players who also didn't have a title, such as Cruyff, Best, and Eusebio. However, as it turns out, he is also regarded in the class of the aforementioned names.

Upon describing Messi, Henry—the former French player and teammate—summed him up well, comparing him with Cristiano

Ronaldo by saying, "When Ronaldo plays, it looks like he's really practiced. When Messi plays, it looks natural." Nothing could be closer to the truth.

As for dribbling, Messi—the kid from Rosario, Argentina, who had the well-known human growth hormone issues and who was signed early on by Barcelona with a contract on a napkin—is not known for fancy step-overs. What he does well comes down to a few things, including turning with the ball, often using the outside of his foot; the pendulum in traffic; and deceptive movements (i.e., he'll dribble one direction, and once the defender commits too far, he turns on a dime the other way with decisive quickness, always keeping the ball nearby). It's all relatively simple, but he does it with greater quickness and speed than opponents, and, most importantly, he has a knack for seeing the right moment to do such things. We'll call it instinct.

When it comes to passing, Messi is great around the box with the give-and-go, where his quickness is used effectively in crowded spaces. While defenders are cautious of his dribbling ability, he has a good eye—and good touch—when it comes to setting up his teammates. In such cases, when he chips the ball, it often has an inner curve to its trajectory, coming off the inside of his foot. The thing about Messi is that he unselfishly goes for goal; he's all too willing to get an assist instead of a score, if it's the right play to make. And that's part of the reason he's such a dangerous player.

Gonzalo Higuain is a classically trained forward who is great finishing around net. He plays as a target up top, often receiving passes and giving them right back to keep the possession going… all the while, waiting for his opportunities around net.

Angel Di Maria has been one of the top wings in world soccer for a few years, using his left foot often to deceive defenders with misdirection; he's a skinny guy and tricky, always changing angles quickly. Possessing the ability to score on his own, pass, or create a situation with dribbling, he is a dangerous player for any opponent.

Ezequiel Lavezzi is a very quick winger with the type of acceleration found in sports cars. He dribbles well and pushes the tempo with opposing defenders.

Javier Mascherano brings a great deal of experience as one of the team's veterans. As a longstanding member of Barcelona, he provides composure on the possession side of the game (a subtle trait in his position which is lacking with most teams that don't get to the quarterfinals). As a central force in defense known for tough play, he anticipates tackles well and often breaks up the momentum of the other team before they can get started.

KEY PLAYER STATS

	Games Played	Goals	Scoring Percentage
Lionel Messi	122	61	50%
Gonzalo Higuain	68	61	45%
Angel Di Maria	90	19	21%
Ezequiel Lavezzi	51	9	17%
Javier Mascherano	139	3	2%

WHAT TO WATCH FOR ON TV—HOW MESSI, NEYMAR, KROOS, AND OTHERS PLAY

The relentless Argentineans are ready to shake things up wherever they play. With every Argentinean team, there's excitement in the air. Watch for a diligent group of players with the pressure of the world on their shoulders, serving a nation that demands victory; they're expected to live up to great teams and players of the past. With every moment, they bring passion. Each goal means the world to them and a nation at home. Like in Brazil, soccer is practically a religion in Argentina.

For the millions of Argentineans that want another title so badly, their representatives—the players on the field—exude that emotion with every kick of the ball. Thanks to the overwhelming pressure after the loss to Chile in the championship of the 2016 Copa America, Messi even retired from the national team for a short time only to be lured back.

The people of Argentina, who have been desperately craving a title since 1986, might want to take solace in the philosophical words of an Argentinean author, Jorge Luis Borges. In a story out of *Everything and Nothing*,* he wrote, "One of the schools of Tlon goes so far as to negate time: it reasons that the present is indefinite, that the future has no reality other than as a present hope, that the past has no reality other than as a present memory."

All their hopes and prayers will be with Messi, leading the attack and getting the ball as often as possible in an effort to stir up

---

* The story is called, "Tlon, Uqbar, Orbis Tertius."

some magic. Outside of that, the supporting players—who are world class in their own right—will combine quick passes during counterattacks and string the passes together with authority during cycles of possession. Each member of the team can shoot with power and placement from around the box, and attacking players have the ability to work their way into the box, causing havoc for opposing defenses.

Their style reflects that of Germany meets Brazil, and they're always one step away from taking over the tournament. Based on past World Cups and their South American qualification journey on route to Russia 2018, which, at times, was hit or miss, it wouldn't be surprising if they won the whole thing or got knocked out in the second round.

That's the story of Argentina and the competitive world of soccer. Unlike international basketball,* international soccer is overwhelmingly competitive, providing a forest of teams that are at the same level, who can win on any given day. Yet Argentina, a team at the front of the pack, is usually one step ahead of most competitors. This is partly why there's so much pressure for them to win it all. Because they can.

Overall Team Rating: 9.4, bordering on 10

---

* Around the world, basketball is improving, but, in many regards, it's a joke, fielding only a handful of competitive teams (the United States, Spain, and Argentina, with a few select others). Why? Because basketball is not the world's game. It's getting close. But not as many people play basketball. Practically every person on earth plays soccer, therefore, making it the heavyweight division of all sports.

Despite their lackluster record in World Cup qualifications, at present, Argentina has too many talented players not to be a 10. However, a team deserving of a 10 theoretically should have had an easier time in qualifications. Also, team chemistry, injuries, and pressure-of-the-moment failures might keep them at a 9.4, but aside from that, they have a roster of 10.

URUGUAY

A BRIEF TEAM HISTORY

World Cup titles: 2 (1930, 1950)

Dating back many years, the small country of Uruguay has a rich tradition of success in soccer. Uruguay was the first team to win the World Cup in 1930, setting the whole parade in motion. However, they didn't compete in 1934 or 1938.

In 1950, twenty years after their first championship, they gained the title again by defeating Brazil on Brazilian soil in front of approximately 200,000 live spectators. For both teams it was a big game, obviously, but for Brazil, it was *the* game for the time. They hadn't won a title yet, and they felt something special happening with the game at large; there was something brewing in Brazil, and they knew it. Uruguay had other plans, and they put Brazil in their place, shutting them down and shutting up the crowd. From there on, for Brazilians, the game became known as "the phantom of '50." Uruguay won the final by a score of 2-1. As a result, they were on top of the world. There had been four World Cups. Italy had two, and Uruguay had two. And, to date, that would be the last time Uruguay would win a World Cup.

In 1954, after beating England in the quarterfinals and losing to Hungary in the semifinals, Uruguay lost to Austria in the consolation match, taking fourth place overall. For the 1958 World Cup, they didn't compete. In 1962, they lost out in group play. Things were better in 1966, as they made the quarterfinals.

World Cup 1970 was even better, as they took fourth place. They beat the USSR in the quarterfinals before losing to Brazil—the eventual champions—in the semis. For the third-place match, they lost to West Germany. They weren't very fortunate in 1974, losing out in group play. For 1978 and 1982, they didn't qualify. In 1986, led by Enzo Francescoli, they were eliminated in the round of 16 by Argentina.

In 1990, they fell to hosts Italy during the round of 16 in Rome in front of over 73,000 fans. For 1994 and 1998, they didn't qualify. Back in the thick of things in 2002, they failed to get out of group play. It was back to the drawing board in 2006, as they didn't qualify.

Then things were looking good again in 2010. Led by the crafty, goal-scoring magic of Luis Suarez and the brilliant creative touch of Diego Forlan, they took first place in their group over Mexico, South Africa, and a disjointed French team. In the round of 16, they defeated South Korea 2-1 with goals from Suarez. In the quarters, they met a talented side from Ghana, who they defeated in penalty kicks. However, they were bested by the Netherlands in the semifinals, which led to another loss to Germany in the third-place match, giving them fourth overall. In 2014, Uruguay lost to Colombia in the round of 16 in the Maracana Stadium—the very place they earned a title back in 1950.

SOUTH AMERICAN COMPETITIONS

Overall, Uruguay has done quite well in the Copa America, winning a total of 15 times in a stretch from 1916 to 2011. With this record, they lead all South American countries. (Argentina rests in second with 14 titles, and Brazil is in third with 8.)

Uruguay has also won the Olympic gold medal in 1924 and 1928.

FACTS ABOUT THEIR COUNTRY

Uruguay is a small country geographically, about the size of Iowa, and in terms of population, with only around 3.4 million people. They have a GDP of around 54 billion. Pilsen and Patricia are popular beers sure to be enjoyed by Uruguayans during the World Cup.

WHERE THE TEAM IS TODAY—TACTICS AND STRATEGIES

Uruguay is coming off of a good 2010 World Cup (still fresh in their minds, anyway), while trying to look past the tribulations of 2014. Despite the flurry of creative genius from their neighbors (Brazil, Argentina, and of late, Chile), Uruguay is struggling to capture the artistic flair in midfield they once had, thanks to players like Forlan and Francescoli.

They're never without solid defenders and a steady one-two punch toward goal, but they're in need of an artistic revival. Will it happen in Russia? That is yet to be seen. However, with the 4-4-2 they'll probably use, they're hoping it arrives sometime in the near future.

ÓSCAR TABÁREZ—A BRIEF COACHING PORTRAIT

Óscar Tabárez—the veteran coach of Uruguay—was born in 1947 in Montevideo, Uruguay. Prior to taking over Uruguay in 2006, Tabárez coached an assortment of teams. As a former defender, his approach is true to Uruguayan tradition: strong defense followed by a flurry of counterattacks along with a steady offensive progression, usually not overtly creative at that.

KEY PLAYERS AND THEIR CHARACTERISTICS

Cristian Rodríguez, Nicolás Lodeiro, and Luis Suárez

Cristian Rodríguez, the rough and tumble veteran midfielder, adds a lot to any lineup with good dribbling, pushing defenses backward, and scoring from a variety of ways, including headers, shots from around the box, and getting into the six-yard area for tap-ins.

Nicolás Lodeiro began playing midfield for the Seattle Sounders in 2016 after a run with the impressive programs of Ajax, Botafogo, Corinthians, and Boca Juniors. As a veteran playmaker, he's known in the US for setting up his Seattle teammates with smart passes into the box and accurate chips to onrushing forwards, like Jordan Morris and Clint Dempsey. In between twisting and turning around defenders, mere obstacles he's left in the dust more than a few times, he's scored a fair share of goals. It's just part of his all-around talent which he brings to Uruguay where he's played since 2009, amassing over 50 caps.

Luis Suárez is a star forward who plays with Barcelona. Previously, he did well with Liverpool. The mild-mannered gentleman is known for discrete temper tantrums from years past (just a few bites here and there; "Naughty-naughty" as Borat would say) before he moves on to score goals. But, since his time at Barcelona, he's become a well-behaved man about town.

Since 2007, he's scored over 45 goals for his country. Argued by many as the best pure forward in the current landscape of international talent, Suárez has a unique ability to create space for himself—just enough of a gap to find a shot on goal. His crafty skill and will to score are attributes that are difficult to teach. Some players possess special gifts around goal that include timing, accuracy, touch, and awareness, and he's definitely one of them. An all-time great forward.

KEY PLAYER STATS

	Games Played	Goals	Scoring Percentage
Cristian Rodríguez	100	11	11%
Nicolás Lodeiro	51	4	7%
Luis Suárez	95	49	51%

WHAT TO WATCH FOR ON TV—HOW MESSI, NEYMAR, KROOS, AND OTHERS PLAY

With Suárez at forward, anything's possible for Uruguay. They will keep things safe defensively, a traditional trait of theirs, and look for opportunities to counter, while working what magic they have around the box to accentuate Suárez's crafty and uncanny gifts around net.

Overall Team Rating: 7, bordering on 7.5

Uruguay lacks midfield ingenuity and positive offensive contributions from their defensive unit; everything can't rest on Suárez.

PERU

A BRIEF TEAM HISTORY

The history of Peruvian soccer is more absent than progressive. Peru competed in the 1930 World Cup, but didn't get out of their group. There was a Peruvian World Cup lull for the next few years. They returned in 1970, reaching the quarterfinals. They didn't make it for 1974. They qualified in 1978 and made it to the second round where they famously were defeated by Argentina 6-0. As for 1982, Peru didn't get past the first round. Since then, they haven't made it back. Until now.

On the road to Russia, Peru placed fifth in South American FIFA World Cup qualifications, just ahead of Chile (who was in sixth place). There were four teams ahead of Peru that had already qualified for Russia. They were Brazil (1), Uruguay (2), Argentina (3), and Colombia (4). As the fifth-place team from South America, Peru had to face the representative from Oceania for a two-game playoff and the chance to make the World Cup. They played New Zealand, and tied the first game 0-0 on November 11, 2017, on the road in Wellington, New Zealand. Then, on November 15, 2017, Peru took it to them, winning 2-0 in front of a home crowd in Lima. In doing so, they were the last team to qualify for Russia 2018.

FACTS ABOUT THEIR COUNTRY

Peru, the land of the ancient Inca, has a population of around 31 million people, with an estimated GDP of 207 billion. It's not often Peru gets to the World Cup. As Peruvian fans watch their team on TV, the parties should be lively. Ajegroup—operating out of Lima, Peru—provides Kola Real (a soda), and for beer, Peruvians have many options, including some beers from the Backus and Johnston Brewery, such as Pilsen Trujillo.

WHERE THE TEAM IS TODAY—TACTICS AND STRATEGIES

Peru possesses good passers that follow a modern-era approach, using short-passing combinations in the midfield to build a progressive attack, while, at the same time, they look for any opportunity to use speed and run at opponents, capitalizing on brisk counterattacks whenever possible. Is their counterattack good enough to earn a place in the semifinals? That might be asking a lot, though they're a competitive team with the ability to catch a higher-ranked team off-guard. They've been known to use a 4-2-3-1 or something of a 4-4-2, and that may stay true or vary just so much, depending on adjustments to their opponent.

RICARDO GARECA—A BRIEF COACHING PORTRAIT

Ricardo Gareca was born in Argentina and played for his national team as a forward from 1981-1986. Since 1996, he has coached a number of teams until landing the job coaching Peru in 2015. His team plays with a brisk approach, exuding offensive flair at every opportunity. Under his guidance, the players should have good confidence after making it through the tough competition of South American qualifications.

KEY PLAYERS AND THEIR CHARACTERISTICS

Jefferson Farfan, Renato Tapia, Christian Cueva, and Edison Flores

Jefferson Farfan, born in 1984, is a veteran attacking player with Peru who made his first national team appearance in 2003. He's an aggressive player with good speed that Peru relies on as a strong presence up top. Since 2017, he's gained experience playing with the Russian team FC Lokomotiv Moscow. Prior to landing in Moscow, he played with a handful of teams, including PSV in the Netherlands; his experience there should help guide Peru with good passing.

Renato Tapia, born in 1995, is a midfielder who has a good presence on defense and had signed with the Dutch side Feyenoord in 2016. He's a younger player, and Peru will count on his energy for success as the tournament carries on.

Christian Cueva was born in 1991 and first played with his home country in 2011. Since then, he's had over 35 caps with a handful of goals. In 2016, he signed with Sao Paulo FC in Brazil where he's done well with a few goals to his name. As a crafty forward with a lot of potential, Peru is hoping to get the most out of him for a strong run in Russia.

Edison Flores, born in 1994, is an attacking player who's been with Peru since 2013. In 2016, he signed with AaB Fodbold in Denmark. His career isn't as old as Gobekli Tepe, but he provides a steady presence up front as a player who can score and get others involved, often with clever one-touch passes in traffic. He's not the fanciest player in the world, but a solid one, which represents much of Peru's lineup.

KEY PLAYER STATS

	Games Played	Goals	Scoring Percentage
Jefferson Farfan	75	22	29%
Renato Tapia	22	2	9%
Christian Cueva	37	7	18%
Edison Flores	21	88	38%

WHAT TO WATCH FOR ON TV—HOW MESSI, NEYMAR, KROOS, AND OTHERS PLAY

Peru has a potent buildup if used the right way. They have a little panache, similar to Argentina, though with somewhat fewer opportunities to score (that is to say, by comparison with top teams like Germany and France). They're an eager team, looking to build on confidence with the ball. Though a concern for them will be how to generate positive scoring chances against the better teams. This will be a salient issue for them as games progress in Russia 2018, as well as other major competitions in the near future. Is Peru a dark horse that can shake the world in Russia? Likely not the case, but, with them, there is potential for a small miracle.

Overall Team Rating: 7.1

Right now, Peru is a solid team that can hold their own with anyone, but, across the board, they lack true offensive consistency.

COLOMBIA

A BRIEF TEAM HISTORY

From 1930-1958, Colombia didn't compete in the World Cup. In 1962, they were eliminated in the group phase. Then, from 1966-1986, they had a long spell of not qualifying. In 1990, they made it to the round of 16, only to be defeated by Cameroon thanks, in part, to a Colombian goalie blunder. In 1994 and 1998, they were eliminated in the group phase. From 2002-2010, they didn't qualify. In 2014, led by James Rodriguez, they had a very good team that made it to the quarterfinals where they were defeated by Brazil.

FACTS ABOUT THEIR COUNTRY

Colombia, the tropical land of fruit and coffee connecting South and Central America, has a population of around 49 million people, with an estimated GDP of 300.9 billion.

Carlos Valderrama—the midfield maestro—has the most caps, with 111. James Rodriquez won the Adidas Golden Boot (i.e., the top scorer) at the 2014 World Cup. Cerveceria Libre is a Colombian beer sure to be enjoyed by people watching their team compete.

WHERE THE TEAM IS TODAY—TACTICS AND STRATEGIES

Colombia is a vibrant, free-flowing group with a ferocious attack. They have a handful of standout talent that can score at any given minute. If anything, they struggle with maintaining consistent chemistry to keep up with the multiple playmakers on the field at any given time. Likely using a 4-4-2, Colombia has an intense attack, currently one of the best in the world.

JOSÉ PÉKERMAN—A BRIEF COACHING PORTRAIT

José Pékerman was born in Argentina and coached his home side from 2004 to 2006, around the beginning of the Messi era. He took over Colombia in 2012. With a group of multitalented players, coach Pékerman's job is to get the ball to all of them, as often as possible. Easier said than done. A lot of their approach is based on a free-wheeling attack they use with a dose of vibrant possession, reflective from time to time of Real Madrid.

KEY PLAYERS AND THEIR CHARACTERISTICS

Pablo Armero, James Rodriguez, Carlos Bacca, and Radamel Falcao

Pablo Armero is a speedster. If you're a coach, and you come across Armero, you get excited thinking of what he can stir up on the left side. Having made his debut with Colombia in 2008, he brings a lot of international experience. Professionally, his talents have been recognized, rightly so, by Udinese, Napoli, West Ham United, AC Milan, and others. Will ten years with Colombia have slowed him down a bit? Possibly. If not, he's a force to reckon with for any defender.

James Rodriguez, born in 1991, is an attacking midfielder who left Colombia to become a star at Real Madrid. His first game for Colombia was in 2011, and since then he's acquired a leadership role on the team, while also scoring big goals in the 2014 World Cup. Maybe he's trapping the ball off his chest, then juggling it with his head before sending it to the ground; or trapping a ground ball into the air for an outstanding goal with a bicycle kick; or passing the ball right on cue for Cristiano Ronaldo or his Colombian teammate, the outstanding Carlos Bacca. Whatever it is, he seems to be doing a lot all the time. While favoring his left foot, he fools opponents with fake kicks and plenty of cutbacks, or changes of direction, setting himself up for either a powerful shot or one with placement and touch with the accuracy of a high-quality finisher.

Carlos Bacca is a forward born in 1986, who signed with AC Milan in 2015. He's been with Colombia since 2010. He can score a variety of ways: headers, a quick release around goal, penalties, dribbling past goalies. He can do it all. Add to that speed and a quick use of the outside of his right foot near goal, catching keepers off-guard (similar to a toe-ball at close range), and the ball's in the back of the net. Above all else, he's a pure goal-scorer.

Radamel Falcao, who's had experience at Manchester United and Chelsea, is a top-flight forward who played his first game with

Colombia in 2007. Whether it's chipping the keeper, blasting it into the upper net, or jumping side volleys, Falcao is one of a kind and one of Colombia's best all-time forwards.

KEY PLAYER STATS

	Games Played	Goals	Scoring Percentage
Pablo Armero	67	2	2%
James Rodriguez	59	21	35%
Carlos Bacca	40	13	32%
Radamel Falcao	70	28	40%

WHAT TO WATCH FOR ON TV—HOW MESSI, NEYMAR, KROOS, AND OTHERS PLAY

The combination play of Armero, Rodriguez, Bacca, and Falcao will light up the tournament and dazzle defenses. Their attacking arsenal is ostensibly boundless, and the only thing holding them back might be bad luck. Other than that, if they're in good form, and injury free, consider Colombia one of the top teams competing on any field in Russia.

Overall Team Rating: 9

NORTH AMERICA (3 ½)

Costa Rica, Mexico, Panama

COSTA RICA

A BRIEF TEAM HISTORY

From 1930-1986, Costa Rica was not in the World Cup. They were nowhere to be found. Then, in 1990, they made an appearance in Italy, getting to the second round where they lost to Czechoslovakia. They were absent in 1994 and 1998 because they didn't qualify. They qualified for the 2002 World Cup but didn't get out of their group. At the 2006 World Cup, they finished last in their group. They didn't qualify for World Cup 2010.

As for Brazil 2014, they fielded a very competitive team that finished first in their group, ahead of Uruguay, Italy, and England. Their good fortune continued by defeating Greece in the second round. But things came to a stop in the quarterfinals, as they lost to the Netherlands.

CONCACAF COMPETITIONS

Costa Rica's inner-CONCACAF journey has been a completely different story than their World Cup tribulations. Historically speaking, Costa Rica is one of the more successful teams out of Central America. Before the United States gained prominence, which was around the 1990s, Mexico and Costa Rica shared dominance over the general territory of CONCACAF.

Costa Rica were champions of the CCCF Championship—a tournament for Central American and Caribbean countries—in 1941, 1946, 1948, 1953, 1955, 1960, and 1961.

For the CONCACAF Championship, held from 1963-1989 (known as the CONCACAF Gold Cup, as of 1991), Costa Rica took home the title in 1963, 1969, and 1989.

The Copa Centroamericana—a smaller tournament for Central American Football Union teams—has yielded success for Costa Rica with plenty of first-place finishes from the 1990s through 2014.

FACTS ABOUT THEIR COUNTRY

Costa Rica is a small country in Central America located between Nicaragua and Panama with a population of about 4.5 million people, and a GDP of around 52 billion.

Soccer is the most popular sport in Costa Rica. Walter Centeno (1995-2009) has the most caps, with 137. Their top goal-scorer is Rolando Fonseca (1992-2011), with 47 goals. As of 2015, Costa Rica went a different direction than most teams and represented New Balance as their uniform sponsor.

Bora is a popular beer sure to be enjoyed during Costa Rica's games.

WHERE THE TEAM IS TODAY—TACTICS AND STRATEGIES

The knock on many Central American teams over the years has been their lack of composure around net. From time to time, many teams from Central America have an inclination to get frantic and rush things. But the Costa Ricans are very patient, skillful, and confident in their approach around the box with touches of brilliance that resemble classic Brazilian stars like Pele from Campbell and a few others. They don't get overly anxious, which allows them to catch traditional powerhouses off-guard.

In the past, they've been known to field a 3-4-2-1, as reported by *SB Nation** on November 15, 2016. Some two years distant, yes, but teams often keep to what has worked. Whether they make subtle or drastic changes for World Cup Russia is yet to be seen. Regardless, for CONCACAF, their overall possession play is good, and, as they've shown in recent years, they fair pretty well within international competition. Their players combine skill and structured passing along with dynamic play from a few individuals, and the result is a dangerous attack.

ÓSCAR RAMÍREZ—A BRIEF COACHING PORTRAIT

Óscar Ramírez played for the Costa Rica national team from 1985-1997. In 2015, he took over the coaching position for his home country, inheriting a great deal of talent with players like Campbell and Ruiz.

---

* Sports Blog Nation.

As a midfielder for Costa Rica, he wasn't a prolific goal-scorer. In fact, his six goals arrived in 1985 (2), 1992 (1), and 1997 (3). Possibly, this patience and keen understanding of the larger picture of the game is what translates to the style of the current squad under his guidance.

KEY PLAYERS AND THEIR CHARACTERISTICS

Joel Campbell and Bryan Ruiz

Joel Campbell has been one of the best individual offensive talents in CONCACAF in recent history. Around the 2014 World Cup, and shortly thereafter, depending who you ask, the argument could be made for him or Clint Dempsey of the United States (with Jesus Corona of Mexico stepping in very recently). Campbell's a very good, instinctive dribbler with great ball skills. Sometimes, what he does is simple, but it always seems to be the right thing and troublesome for the opposing team. Dempsey, free of injury, has the same quality; both players, regardless of the situation, ostensibly do the right thing for the given moment, and it always seems to move the play along in a positive way, which other players just can't duplicate.

Bryan Ruiz is similar to Campbell in that when he does something on the field, there seems to be a positive effect in the immediate aftermath. The possession gets better, or another teammate is given a perfect pass in front of goal a few plays later; he's one of those "there's always something going on when he's around the ball" kind of players.

KEY PLAYER STATS

	Games Played	Goals	Scoring Percentage
Joel Campbell	70	14	20%
Bryan Ruiz	101	23	22%

WHAT TO WATCH FOR ON TV—HOW MESSI, NEYMAR, KROOS, AND OTHERS PLAY

Costa Rica is very good at connecting passes to players in forward movement. Campbell is dangerous around the corners of the box, while Ruiz supplements this attack with his awareness of the field. They're a solid combination, and their supporting cast is a group to be reckoned with. Should any underdog team make a surprise run, expect Costa Rica to be at the top of that list.

Overall Team Rating: 7.8

MEXICO

A BRIEF TEAM HISTORY

In 1930, Mexico was knocked out of the first ever World Cup in the group phase. In 1934, they didn't qualify. They didn't participate in 1938. For World Cups 1950, 1954, 1958, 1962, and 1966, Mexico was eliminated in the group stage. By 1970, as hosts, they improved, making it to the quarterfinals where they lost to Italy. In 1974, they didn't qualify; in 1978, they were eliminated in the group stage; and for 1982, they again didn't qualify.

As hosts, yet again, in 1986, their luck in the world's largest tournament was going to improve. They were recovering from a major earthquake prior to the tournament, and, as it turned out, the World Cup was a great motivational force to get the nation back on its feet again. Led by Hugo Sanchez, one of their most notorious forwards, Mexico played very well, leading their group which consisted of Paraguay, Belgium, and Iraq.

They drew a massive audience. Their opener—a 2-1 victory over Belgium—was held in the Estadio Azteca Stadium in front of an estimated 110,000 people, and the crowd chanted, "Mexico…Mexico!" Then, in front of over 114,000 people, they defeated Bulgaria in the second round. But, upon reaching the quarterfinals, they switched venues from Mexico City to Monterrey and lost to West Germany in front of approximately 41,000 spectators. Mexico didn't compete in 1990.

Then came the second-round blues. For World Cups 1994, 1998, 2002, 2006, 2010, and 2014, they were eliminated in the round of 16. Based on this record, it may seem as though Mexico will take many years to win the World Cup. They are certainly hoping to raise the trophy sooner, and Russia 2018 represents a perfect opportunity.

CONCACAF COMPETITIONS

Within the realm of CONCACAF, Mexico has a rich tradition of winning. They've won multiple championships in the CONCACAF Championship (held from 1963-1989) and the Gold Cup (1991 to the present), including in 1965, 1971, 1977, 1993, 1996, 1998, 2003, 2009, 2011 and 2015.

As of 2017, Mexico placed fourth in the Confederations Cup in Russia.

FACTS ABOUT THEIR COUNTRY

Mexico—one of the world's ultimate vacation destinations—has a population of approximately 119 million people, with a GDP of around 1.2 trillion.

Mexico's most capped player is Claudio Suarez, who played for the national team from 1992-2006 in a total of 177 games. Mexico is a festive place. Like Brazil, the United States, and many other countries, they have designated places for people to gather en masse to watch World Cup games on a big screen. In many ways, it's like being at the stadium. Wherever the location may be, Corona is a popular beer that will be out and about while people gather for games on TV.

WHERE THE TEAM IS TODAY—TACTICS AND STRATEGIES

Since around 2012, Mexico is said to have one of their best teams of all time. Some of the cast of players has included Guardado, Chicharito, Marquez, Jesus Corona, and Giovani dos Santos. And, this particular group of guys hit their peak around the 2016 Copa America, despite taking an embarrassing defeat from Chile.

They've used a 4-2-3-1 in the past, as reported by *SB Nation* on November 11, 2016. Many teams stay with the same formation for years, and this may persist with Mexico, depending on the coach's vibe going into Russia. Whichever formation Mexico applies, they should be a strong team to contend with. They have sound possession and the ability to slow the game down, while using their explosive speed when necessary.

JUAN CARLOS OSORIO—A BRIEF COACHING PORTRAIT

Juan Carlos Osorio took the Mexican coaching job in 2015 after coaching a number of professional teams, including the New York Red Bulls and the Chicago Fire of the MLS.

He was born in Colombia, and as a midfielder, he played for three professional teams from 1982-1987, including Deportivo Pereira in Colombia, Internacional in Brazil, and Once Caldas in Colombia.

It's no secret that Mexico has been known to change coaches as frequently as a load of laundry. Osorio has inherited a team of super talent, which any coach would get excited over. His main objective is to keep the counterattack, which is strong, in place and push the players to remain patient with a sound approach they've developed in the possession end of the game, thanks, in part, to the on-field guidance of longtime veteran Raphael Marquez.

KEY PLAYERS AND THEIR CHARACTERISTICS

Andres Guardado, Hector Herrera, Oribe Peralta, Javier Hernandez, and Jesus Corona

Andres Guardado is a winger and midfielder, a veteran who possesses quickness and a good left foot. Much of Mexico's spark is based on his sweeping midfield activity.

Hector Herrera is a gifted central midfielder and playmaker who possesses uncanny skill with touch passes. Some players have a knack to organize a team. That would be Herrera. Great vision. Great facilitator. He's arguably the best passer of the ball in North America. But his passes are usually very subtle and nuanced. He's definitely one to watch. He's constantly making things work for his team in ways that aren't quantified by stats.

Oribe Peralta is a defined, aggressive, and confident goal-scorer. Often overshadowed by the popularity of Chicharito, Peralta is arguably a more able finisher around the net.

Javier Hernandez, also known affectionately as Chicharito, is a well-versed scoring threat for Mexico. As a veteran player, he's had experience with top clubs around the world, including Bayer Leverkusen, Real Madrid, and Manchester United. Not the most elusive dribbler, he's a crafty passer and has a knack for finding the right place to be around net.

Jesus Corona, born in 1993, is a relatively new star on the Mexican scene, but one that has quickly made a strong impression as a permanent icon. He has a gifted dribbling ability, which he uses well to create scoring chances around the box.

KEY PLAYER STATS

	Games Played	Goals	Scoring Percentage
Andres Guardado	140	24	17%
Hector Herrera	62	5	8%
Oribe Peralta	62	25	40%
Javier Hernandez	98	49	50%
Jesus Corona	32	7	21%

WHAT TO WATCH FOR ON TV—HOW MESSI, NEYMAR, KROOS, AND OTHERS PLAY

This crop of Mexican players is probably one of the best groups in recent Mexican history, if not the most talented of all time. They are overwhelmingly loaded with offensive talent that has good on-field chemistry together. They possess the ball remarkably well with an intuition to get forward in dangerous places around their opponent's goal.

From Guardado to Hernandez to Corona, it's all strung together by their total appreciation of the ball and the subtle guidance—with a touch of brilliance—from the middleman, Herrera.

Overall Team Rating: 8

Mexico has too much offensive power to be anything less than an 8. On paper, they're more like an 8.5 or 8.8, but one setback is based on their terrible response to the shellacking they took from Chile in the 2016 Copa America. How a team takes defeat is indicative of how they'll persevere during big moments down the road.

PANAMA

A BRIEF TEAM HISTORY

From 1930 to...who are we kidding? Before Russia 2018, Panama had never gotten to the World Cup. This is their very first one! And they are excited, to put it lightly.

During the closing months of 2017, amid the 2018 World Cup qualification run in CONCACAF, Panama stood their ground during the Hexagonal competition, eventually taking third place ahead of Honduras, the United States, and Trinidad and Tobago.

CENTRAL AMERICAN SUCCESS

Panama became champions of the 1951 CCCF Championship (a competition for Central American and Caribbean teams). They also won the Copa Centroamericana in 2009.

FACTS ABOUT THEIR COUNTRY

Panama, the land of the Panama Canal, has a population of around 4 million people, with an estimated GDP of 47 billion.

One of their well-known athletes is the boxer, Roberto Duran, the Hands of Stone. He had many great fights in the 80s with "Sugar" Ray Leonard, "Marvelous" Marvin Hagler, and Tommy "the Hitman" Hearns. However, soccer is Panama's number one sport.

While people hover around TV screens for Panama's first World Cup, they will likely have Atlas, Soberana, Panama, or Balboa beer to drink.

WHERE THE TEAM IS TODAY—TACTICS AND STRATEGIES

Even playing at home, Panama should do better. At times, they seem like a real national team. Then, without much warning, they abandon skill and technique, looking less like a World Cup-bound team and more like a group of guys that need serious practice. Practice would be code for starting with the basics. How they can be so off with their touch and general understanding of the game is puzzling. Of course, the argument could be made that the first team may not always be available. With that said, at the national level, any and every player should be prepared with exceptional skill. (You would think.) So, for Panama to oscillate from an acceptable team at the national level, which they are from time to time, to a lackluster group of amateurs is absolutely astounding. It seems more often than not the majority of players in any given lineup need work on their technique in regards to passing, trapping, and dribbling. Very little looks natural.

They typically play a 4-4-2 with a lot of emphasis on getting the ball into the box. But often, they lack numbers around goal, along with continuity in passing structure.

HERNAN DARIO GOMEZ—A BRIEF COACHING PORTRAIT

Hernan Dario Gomez was born in 1956 in Colombia. He played professionally with Independiente Medellin and Atletico Nacional, both in Colombia. He also coached Colombia (twice), Ecuador, and Guatemala before taking the job with Panama in 2014.

To put things mildly, Panama needs something of a miracle to be considered a World Cup contender. Can Panama's defense be blamed? Simple answer: yes. Then, offensively, you get into tactical dilemmas. *Why did he just do that? What was he thinking?* Then, as the camera pans past their coach, you might start thinking: *How on earth will he ever defeat Brazil or Germany?* But, in the coach's defense, they have moments of brilliance, like any team. However, in the long run, they are very inferior to top talent from around the world. To completely blame coach Gomez isn't fair. There are clearly issues within their system at large, from coaching youth players to transitioning to pro. But, with athletic guys at his disposal, there's much more the coach could've done with this group, and basic skill training would be a good start.

KEY PLAYERS AND THEIR CHARACTERISTICS

Gabriel Gomez, Armando Cooper, and Luis Tejada

Gabriel Gomez has played with a ton of teams, including the Philadelphia Union in 2012. Since 2003, he has attained valuable club experience along with over 125 caps for his national team, which is a great asset for Panama in Russia.

Armando Cooper—a midfielder with experience at Toronto FC—should bring a strong work ethic to the lineup, along with serviceable passing in transition.

Luis Tejada is a forward who has a lot of experience with a number of teams, including Al Ain in the United Arab Emirates (2005), Real Salt Lake in the MLS (2007), along with Toluca in Mexico (2012-2013). He's a goal-scorer that looks for opportunities to capitalize on his opponents' mistakes around the goal.

KEY PLAYER STATS

	Games Played	Goals	Scoring Percentage
Gabriel Gomez	136	11	8%
Armando Cooper	82	6	7%
Luis Tejada	104	43	41%

WHAT TO WATCH FOR ON TV—HOW MESSI, NEYMAR, KROOS, AND OTHERS PLAY

Panama is a team searching for brilliance with every touch on the ball, every possession. They might find it every once in a while, but all in all they're going to push the ball toward goal quickly, desperately looking for "get rich quick schemes" in terms of scoring.

Overall Team Rating: 6, leaning toward 5.9

AFRICA (5)

Egypt, Morocco, Nigeria, Senegal, Tunisia

A quick note on African competitions:

Africa Cup of Nations

First tournament: 1957

African Nations Championship

First tournament: 2009

EGYPT

A BRIEF TEAM HISTORY

Egypt was not present for the 1930 World Cup in Uruguay. In 1934, they lost early in the group phase, placing thirteenth overall. After a long wait, they reemerged in 1990. But, they didn't get out of their group. Since then, they haven't qualified. Until now.

On the road to Russia, Egypt got first in their group which consisted of Uganda, Ghana, and Congo. Egypt is looking to take this experience into Russia 2018, hoping to become the first African team to make the semifinals of a World Cup.

AFRICAN COMPETITIONS

Egypt has done much better on the African continent. They are the leading team with championships in the Africa Cup of Nations. They've won it seven times in 1957, 1959, 1986, 1998, 2006, 2008, and 2010.

FACTS ABOUT THEIR COUNTRY

Egypt—the land of pyramids, pharaohs, and ancient mystery— has a population of about 92.8 million people, with a GDP of around 330 billion. Ahmed Hassan—who played for his country from 1995-2012—leads all Egyptian players in caps with 184. Luxor, Sakara, and many other choices from the land of ancient beer are available for Egyptians as they watch their team on TV.

WHERE THE TEAM IS TODAY—TACTICS AND STRATEGIES

Egypt typically fields a 4-3-3 with a quick attack. They also have a tough defense, and they constantly test their opponent, pushing the issue and looking for goals. Egypt's chances of winning the World Cup are not great, but they're a contender…somewhere in the middle-of-the-pack. Based on their success in Africa, they have solid potential. After all, along with Cameroon and Nigeria, they've consistently been regarded as one of Africa's best teams. However, to win the entire World Cup in Russia they'll need something special, something on the order of 1,618 calls in their favor. But that's not to say they don't have a chance to do well. Egypt has a soccer program steadily growing in quality, and they have a chance to represent Africa in a big way.

They have many things going in their favor. They consistently produce teams adept on both sides of the ball. Their players have skill and good experience at the club level. With that said, it wouldn't be much of a surprise to see Egypt make a few upsets in World Cup 2018.

HECTOR CUPER—A BRIEF COACHING PORTRAIT

Hector Cuper, who was born in Argentina, has been coaching since 1993 with an assortment of teams, including Parma in Italy; he took the Egypt gig in 2015. Prior to providing expertise from the sideline, he played three games as a defender for Argentina in 1984.

His approach with Egypt includes the 4-3-3 (unless changes occur last minute) with a lot of movement defensively from the outside forwards, often getting back to help out. Under his guidance, the team moves well as a group, and they have a lot of potential should they stay consistent.

KEY PLAYERS AND THEIR CHARACTERISTICS

Mohamed Elneny, Mohamed Salah, Abdallah Said, and Ahmed Fathy

Mohamed Elneny is a defensive midfielder who signed with Arsenal in 2016. He first played with Egypt in 2011. Not a big goal-scorer, he's the guy in the middle of the field, churning things out defensively, applying pressure to opponents, and creating the loose balls, which complement his practical contributions on offense.

Mohamed Salah, born in 1992, is a forward who has been with Egypt since 2011. After spending time with Chelsea and other teams, he signed with Roma in 2016 where he's been charging down the field in the Serie A. He's a left-footer who dominates the line with surging runs, attacking the open space and creating dangerous situations in the box.

Abdallah Said, who has played with Egypt since 2008, has a strong right foot, always a threat around the box. He's struck home over 35 goals with Al Ahly SC (founded in 1907), the Egyptian club out of Cairo.

Ahmed Fathy, born in 1984, is an experienced defender and leader on the team who Egypt is counting on as a guiding presence on the backline.

KEY PLAYER STATS

	Games Played	Goals	Scoring Percentage
Mohamed Elneny	57	5	8%
Mohamed Salah	56	32	57%
Abdallah Said	30	6	20%
Ahmed Fathy	120	3	2%

WHAT TO WATCH FOR ON TV—HOW MESSI, NEYMAR, KROOS, AND OTHERS PLAY

Egypt brings a fervent approach to each contest…a little two-man game and a lot of counterattacking. They go after teams with a high tempo and a lot of speed, getting Salah and Said involved up front with quick passing and aggressive runs toward goal. Should there be a large contingent of Egyptian fans at the games, when the team scores, they erupt like a sonic boom.

Overall Team Rating: 7.3

MOROCCO

A BRIEF TEAM HISTORY

From 1930-1966, Morocco didn't compete in the World Cup. Morocco's first World Cup appearance was in Mexico in 1970. In that tournament they lost out in the group phase.

They'd have to wait until 1986—back in Mexico—for their next shot at it. With a few amazing goals from Abderrazak Khairi, they had a good showing, winning their group which got them to the round of 16. Waiting for them was West Germany, and that would be the end of 1986 for Morocco. It wasn't until 1994 and 1998 that Morocco had another run at the World Cup, losing out in the group phase in both tournaments. And they haven't been back since.

In the African World Cup qualification games—which concluded in late 2017—Morocco's group consisted of Cote d'Ivoire, Gabon, and Mali. With 12 points, Morocco finished in first place, earning a place in the 2018 World Cup, which represents their twenty-year return.

OTHER COMPETITIONS

Morocco's big moment in the history of soccer came in 1976 when they won the Africa Cup of Nations, which was hosted in Ethiopia that year. They also won the 2012 Arab Nations Cup.

FACTS ABOUT THEIR COUNTRY

Morocco, situated on the northwest corner of Africa and connected to Spain and Europe, is the land of Casablanca, coast-side casinos, mystery, and the ancient archaeological site of Volubilis. It has a population of around 33 million people, with an estimated GDP of 103 billion.

WHERE THE TEAM IS TODAY—TACTICS AND STRATEGIES

Morocco is a team trying to get into the mix. They've had sporadic moments over the years, and their hope is to continue on a path to further success. The 2018 World Cup offers them a great opportunity to give the newer generations a taste of the grand prize.

Likely operating out of a 4-4-2, Morocco has quick players on defense, while offensively they tend to keep defenders wide in possession and pursue the wings in the attack often.

HERVÉ RENARD—A BRIEF COACHING PORTRAIT

Morocco's coach is the French-born Hervé Renard. He took over the post in 2016 after coaching various teams, including Zambia, Angola, and Ivory Coast. His team has the ability to calm the game down with thoughtful passing; though, Renard's biggest challenge will likely end up having to do with keeping the players composed during possession if they go down a goal, particularly against better teams with more World Cup experience.

KEY PLAYERS AND THEIR CHARACTERISTICS

Younes Belhanda, Mbark Boussoufa, and Hakim Ziyech

Born in 1990, Younes Belhanda is a talented and acrobatic midfielder who can put the ball in the back of the net as well as set up teammates with thoughtful passes. He's had experience with Dynamo Kyiv (Ukraine) and Nice. His first game with Morocco came in 2010. As a veteran, he'll be counted on for a surge down the stretch.

Mbark Boussoufa, born in 1984 in the Netherlands, is veteran midfielder who brings timely experience from his days with the Belgian side, Anderlecht, among others.

Hakim Ziyech is a forward who signed with Ajax in 2016. Prior to that, he had experience with the Dutch teams FC Twente and SC Heerenveen. Whether it's volleying from outside the box, dribbling past three players for a goal, or wheeling and dealing around the wing, he's a scoring threat. In his relatively short stint with Morocco (which began in 2015), he's gotten off to a good start, going into the final months of 2017 with a scoring percentage of 63%. Morocco will look to expand this trend going into Russia.

KEY PLAYER STATS

	Games Played	Goals	Scoring Percentage
Younes Belhanda	32	3	9%
Mbark Boussoufa	54	7	12%
Hakim Ziyech	11	7	63%

WHAT TO WATCH FOR ON TV—HOW MESSI, NEYMAR, KROOS, AND OTHERS PLAY

Morocco will be an interesting team to watch as they possess the ball calmly with many players equipped with European club experience. Will they be able to remain on their game is another question altogether. Not much is expected of them, and to get out of their group should be done with some effort. Are they a dark horse team that might take the tournament—and world— by surprise? Most likely, no. However, they have a few things going in their favor, including an experienced coach, some crafty players, and a streak of confidence coming out of a tough African qualification run leading into the 2018 World Cup.

Overall Team Rating: 7.0

NIGERIA

A BRIEF TEAM HISTORY

From 1930-1990, Nigeria didn't compete in the World Cup. Not once. In the 1994 World Cup, they made their debut. Finally. They actually finished atop their group, ahead of Bulgaria, Argentina, and Greece, with goals from Yekini, Amokachi, Amunike, Siasia, and George. In the round of 16, despite going up a goal by Amunike, they reached the end thanks to a loss to Italy with a late goal to tie from Roberto Baggio followed by a penalty kick to push the Italians ahead.

In France 1998, like four years earlier, Nigeria finished atop their group, ahead of Paraguay, Spain, and Bulgaria, with two wins and a loss. In the second round, a goal from Babangida wouldn't be enough, and they lost 4-1 to Denmark.

At the 2002 World Cup, they didn't get out of their group. They didn't make it to Germany 2006. Again, in 2010, they repeated their history from eight years earlier, and didn't get out of their group. In 2014, they had better luck, making it to the round of 16; though, ultimately, they were defeated 2-0 by France with a goal from Pogba and an own goal from Joseph Yobo.

On the road to Russia, Nigeria had to go through an African qualification group which consisted of Zambia, Cameroon, and Algeria. Nigeria has a talented team going into Russia 2018, ready to make a big impression.

AFRICAN COMPETITIONS

Nigeria's had good fortune in the Africa Cup of Nations, taking first place in 1980, 1994, and 2013.

OLYMPIC SUCCESS

Nigeria has had good Olympic success, taking the gold medal for soccer in 1996.

FACTS ABOUT THEIR COUNTRY

Nigeria, a West African country, has a population of around 188 million people, with an approximate GDP of 484 billion. As a nation, they were declared and recognized in 1960, while declaring Republic status in 1963. They are an oil-rich land with strong ties to European Union leaders and OPEC-related entities.

The Nigeria national team coach of 1949 was Jack Finch, who played professionally at Fulham from 1930-1946. For game-watching parties, Nigerians have an assortment of beers to choose from, including Turbo King Stout and Legend Extra Stout.

WHERE THE TEAM IS TODAY—TACTICS AND STRATEGIES

Nigeria, as one of Africa's best teams, has a so-so chance to win the World Cup. Like most, they're middle of the pack. They implement a 4-4-2, which at times looks like a 4-1-4-1, but that's what happens when players shuffle around.

Essentially, they can keep up defensively and hold games to a tight score. On the offensive end, they have the capability for a patient buildup, which, from time to time, they use to their advantage, taking hold of any opportunity to fly at opponents with a quick counter.

Though, at times, they put themselves into situations where they force their hand unnecessarily. It's one of those situations shared by many teams: *good pass, good pass, good pass, everything's looking good*, and at this point someone thinks they have to push an awkward ball into traffic, which is their downfall. (It's an awkward phenomenon suffered by many middle-of-the-pack teams—someone just has to push an awkward, clumsy, nervous pass into traffic with no backup plan. Egypt falls into the same category. Brazil, Argentina, and other top teams do the same thing as well, but less often, which is partly an essential key to their success.) Should Nigeria continue to be patient and not force things as much, better results will come their way, thus pushing them into the upper part of the middle-of-the-pack teams. Right now, they're in the middle part, along with Egypt and Costa Rica, to name a few.

SALISU YUSUF—A BRIEF COACHING PORTRAIT

Salisu Yusuf, born in Nigeria, was made head coach in 2016. Gernot Rohr, of German descent, was appointed technical advisor as of 2016. Under Coach Yusuf's direction, Nigeria presses heavy with their outside mids. They keep their shape fairly well, and, with a solid roster, they intend on making a big move in Russia.

KEY PLAYERS AND THEIR CHARACTERISTICS

Elderson Echiejile, Ogenyi Onazi, Ahmed Musa, and Victor Moses

Elderson Echiejile is a veteran defender who plays a role on the team of *keeping things simple* by clearing out the danger, holding the opposing team to as close to zero as possible, and setting up attacking players with outlet passes that are beneficial to their upfield momentum.

Ogenyi Onazi is a midfielder found in the middle who is a playmaker in the guise of Pirlo; he's good with the dribble in small spaces, creating space for a simple outlet to continue possession or a telling through pass to an onrushing forward. And, like Pirlo, the chances of him scoring a goal are very low; in Onazi's case, it's about as likely as a UFO sighting.

Ahmed Musa, a 5'7" forward, signed with Leicester City in 2016. Previously, he was with CSKA Moscow from 2012-2016, where he scored 42 goals. He's an engaging forward that can turn on the speed and really create danger for an opposing team.

Victor Moses rounds up the attack, bringing a lot of experience from the EPL with Chelsea and a handful of other English teams, including Crystal Palace, Wigan Athletic, Liverpool, Stoke City, and West Ham United. He sparkles the field with skill, dribbling ability in tight spaces, elusive moves around the sidelines, and he is also equipped with a strong shot that makes headaches for goalies. Given a little time on the ball, Victor Moses will likely make something happen.

KEY PLAYER STATS

	Games Played	Goals	Scoring Percentage
Elderson Echiejile	57	2	3%
Ogenyi Onazi	48	1	2%
Ahmed Musa	63	13	20%
Victor Moses	28	10	35%

WHAT TO WATCH FOR ON TV—HOW MESSI, NEYMAR, KROOS, AND OTHERS PLAY

The Nigerian players have a lot of European club experience, which gives them poise in possession as they work the ball around the backline. In terms of scoring, they have a vibrant attack, which is spread out, coming from players like Musa and Moses, guys that have a lot of speed, flair, and ingenuity around the goal.

Overall Team Rating: 7.4

SENEGAL

A BRIEF TEAM HISTORY

Senegal's first World Cup was in 2002, where they did well, making it as far as the quarterfinals. Russia 2018 is their first trip back. On their way to the 2018 World Cup, during the Preliminary Competition, Senegal got first place in their group over Burkina Faso, Cape Verde Islands, and South Africa.

FACTS ABOUT THEIR COUNTRY

Senegal's population is a little over 15 million people, with an estimated GDP of 16 billion. It's a small country in West Africa, neighboring Mauritania, Mali, the Gambia, and Guinea-Bissau.

A popular beer in Senegal is 33 Export, which should make the rounds big time as the World Cup plays out and Senegal makes a run for glory.

WHERE THE TEAM IS TODAY—TACTICS AND STRATEGIES

Senegal's formation will likely be a 4-4-2. Defensively, they have some quickness and will look to exploit pressure on the ball to create turnovers. Offensively, they're a team trying to find a rhythm, though sometimes the process can get a little jumbled.

With one World Cup in 2002 and a few decent results at the Africa Cup of Nations, Senegal is a team looking for a big moment. It could be successfully argued that a quarterfinal run in the 2002 World Cup was a big moment, which it was for a first-time appearance, but they are looking for much bigger accomplishments to get things moving for a great West African soccer program. They're definitely not a world power, but should they ever get there, this is the beginning portion of their journey.

ALIOU CISSE—A BRIEF COACHING PORTRAIT

Aliou Cisse, who was born in 1976 in Senegal, played for a number of teams in his day, including Lille and Birmingham City. He also played for Senegal from 1999 to 2005. As a coach, he took over the team in 2015. Since then, his mission has been to get Senegal back to the World Cup, and that he did. Under his guidance (with a team that comes across as "Nigeria's protégé"), watch for Senegal to use their underdog status to their advantage.

KEY PLAYERS AND THEIR CHARACTERISTICS

Moussa Sow, Idrissa Gueye, and Kara Mbodji

Moussa Sow is a French-born forward who has played with Lille (among others), and first joined Senegal in 2009. He's scored a number of goals for his country, and he'll be depended upon for leadership throughout Russia.

Idrissa Gueye, born in 1989, signed with the big English club Everton in 2016. As a midfielder with Senegal, he attained his first cap in 2011 and looks to bring both his EPL and international experience to the high-pressure games of World Cup Russia.

Kara Mbodji will be holding things down as a center defender on the backline, trying to get a shutout. He signed with the Belgian side Anderlecht in 2015 and has managed to score a few goals there. His all-around contribution will be vital for Senegal to move forward in Russia 2018.

KEY PLAYER STATS

	Games Played	Goals	Scoring Percentage
Moussa Sow	45	18	40%
Idrissa Gueye	46	1	2%
Kara Mbodji	49	4	8%

WHAT TO WATCH FOR ON TV—HOW MESSI, NEYMAR, KROOS, AND OTHERS PLAY

Senegal will bring a lot of energy, passion, and optimism. With an assortment of players who have European club experience, they have a sufficient amount of poise on the ball, though not without a few mishaps here and there. Currently, they come across as a less potent Nigerian squad. Unless luck is heavily on their side, they'll have a hard time getting out of their group.

Overall Team Rating: 6.8

TUNISIA

A BRIEF TEAM HISTORY

From 1930 to 1974, Tunisia didn't compete in a World Cup. In 1978, they made their debut in Argentina, but didn't get out of their group which consisted of Poland, West Germany, and Mexico. Their next World Cup was 1998, when they couldn't get out of their group. The same occurred in the 2002 and 2006 World Cups.

During the African World Cup qualification games—referred to as "Preliminary Competition" by FIFA—the Tunisians got first in their group, which consisted of Congo DR, Libya, and Guinea.

OTHER COMPETITIONS

Tunisia won the Africa Cup of Nations in 2004. They won the Arab Nations Cup in 1963.

FACTS ABOUT THEIR COUNTRY

Tunisia's population is around 10.9 million people, with an estimated GDP of 42 billion. Tunisia's most capped player is

Radhi Jaidi, with 105. Celtia and Berber beer are likely to make the rounds during Tunisia's games, as people back home watch their team try for an upset in Russia.

WHERE THE TEAM IS TODAY—TACTICS AND STRATEGIES

Tunisia plays some hybrid of a 4-3-3. By design, or accidentally, they sway around, often keeping players close together like swarming sharks while sometimes forming a defensive backline of five defenders. While in possession of the ball, they sometimes leave three defenders back—usually while they're in possession—and then as things progress, it all takes the shape of a 4-3-3, more or less.

NABIL MAALOUL—A BRIEF COACHING PORTRAIT

Nabil Maaloul took the responsibility of coaching in 2017. He coached the team before in 2013, while also serving as an assistant in the past. The Tunisian-born Maaloul also coached Kuwait from 2014-2017. With Tunisia, he's inherited an uphill task, taking the team on during the end of qualifications, only one year before the World Cup. His vision should be to keep the team operating at a skillful level, with a bit of improvement on their short passing combinations—which fits their style—before they hit their stride in World Cup action.

KEY PLAYERS AND THEIR CHARACTERISTICS

Mohamed Amine Ben Amor, Ahmed Akaichi, and Taha Yassine Khenissi

Mohamed Amine Ben Amor is an able-footed midfielder who joined Tunisia in 2015. He plays sturdy and relentless, holding the fort with good passes and thoughtful play.

Ahmed Akaichi, born in 1989, is a forward who's played with Tunisia since 2010. He's a serviceable attacking player that will bring experience and leadership, which will be valuable for the success of Tunisia's efforts on the big stage.

Taha Yassine Khenissi, born in 1992, is a forward with quick moves around the box and a mind for scoring. Since joining Tunisia in 2013, he's contributed toward their success and will be an asset with the team in Russia.

KEY PLAYER STATS

	Games Played	Goals	Scoring Percentage
Mohamed Amine Ben Amor	22	2	9%
Ahmed Akaichi	29	9	31%
Khenissi	20	5	25%

WHAT TO WATCH FOR ON TV—HOW MESSI, NEYMAR, KROOS, AND OTHERS PLAY

The Tunisians with Mohamed Amine Ben Amor, Ahmed Akaichi, Taha Yassine Khenissi, and others will look to play short passes with a lot of crafty skill as they attack through the middle. Their wide game is less active but nonetheless a part of their movement downfield. A good team that relies on skill, short passing, and ingenuity, Tunisia is a group to watch in Russia and beyond.

Overall Team Rating: 7.0

ASIA (4 ½)

Australia, Iran, Japan, Saudi Arabia, South Korea

AUSTRALIA

A BRIEF TEAM HISTORY

Prior to Russia 2018, Australia has only competed in four World Cups: 1974, 2006, 2010, and 2014. Their entries have left less than exciting results, notwithstanding the hurrah of 2006 when they made it to the round of 16. They hope to change things for the better in Russia.

On the road to Russia, in the Asian World Cup qualification rounds during the final months of 2017, Australia finished third in their group (Group B) behind Japan and Saudi Arabia. According to FIFA's rules, Australia went into a playoff with Syria (who finished third in their group) to see who would represent Asia in the continental playoff against the representative from CONCACAF. Australia won the two-game contest over Syria by a total (or aggregate) score of 3-2.

After doing so, Australia went on to play Honduras—who was the fourth-place finisher out of North America—for a chance at going to Russia 2018. The first of two playoff games was a 0-0 tie on November 10, 2017, on the road in Honduras. A few days later, on November 15, 2017, the second and final game was a 3-1 victory for the Aussies, played in Sydney, Australia. With that, after a hard-fought qualification road, Australia earned a place in Russia 2018.

ASIAN COMPETITIONS

Australia has won a few tournaments in their area, including the AFC Asian Cup in 2015. Aside from that, they were OFC* Nations Cup champions in 1980, 1996, 2000, and 2004.

FACTS ABOUT THEIR COUNTRY

Australia—the land of exotic adventures Down Under—has around 24 million people, and a GDP of about 1.2 trillion.

The Asian Football Confederation honored Australia as Team of the Year in 2006 and 2015. The goalie, Mark Schwarzer (1993-2013), has the most caps, with 109. (He played professionally with a number of teams, including Leicester City, Chelsea, and Fulham.) To be sure, many people watching the World Cup games from Australia will be enjoying Foster's and many other beers.

WHERE THE TEAM IS TODAY—TACTICS AND STRATEGIES

Without the white birds that often fly around the field during home games, Australia might not feel at home in Russia. Aside from that, Australia has a very small chance of winning the World

---

* Oceania Football Confederation.

Cup. They've been knocking on the door of world soccer for the better part of fifteen years or so. They, along with teams like the US, Cameroon, and Saudi Arabia, have been getting better each World Cup, it seems...even if their World Cup record might not show it.

The Aussies employ a style similar to their parent nation, England. Call it the EPL Light. While at the same time, they're essentially employing the approach of Spain, with attempts at a well-thought-out, short-passing attack. They're strong on defense, with athletic guys that challenge well for aerial balls and look for contact in tackles.

Going with a 4-3-3 (which is what they'll likely use, keeping defenders very wide during possession), they're definitely not going to showcase the short-passing wizardry of a team like Spain. Nor are they going to dazzle anyone with dribbling exploits you might see with Argentina or Brazil. They're strong in the air, relying on crosses for much of their attack. The players tend to be well built and play aggressive balls down the line, pushing their opponent into a corner where they use isolation situations to their advantage. They're more about team play than individual flair, and this benefits their chances any time they take the field, as their sole focus is to keep their opponent off the scoreboard, which they do fairly well, while they plug away, trying to get numbers into the box offensively.

As soccer has become more popular Down Under, and as their national team has gained much needed confidence from three consecutive World Cup appearances, they're getting more accustomed to using their skillset and doing well on the biggest stage.

Like South Korea, Australia is improving on a sound buildup in their attack, but they lack individual ingenuity. They lack a creative pulse, which will, for all intents and purposes, hold them back from progressing very far in Russia 2018 and World Cups in the near future.

ANGE POSTECOGLOU—A BRIEF COACHING PORTRAIT

Ange Postecoglou spent his playing days with South Melbourne and Western Suburbs, also playing with the Australian national team in 1986. He began coaching in 1996, mainly in Australia, with a stint in Greece, and took over the Australian men's national team in 2013. Under his direction, the team has taken big steps in getting to a better place as a program. They're growing with confidence each World Cup cycle, which has a lot to do with adopting a sound approach to passing combinations, very popular in the modern playing era.

KEY PLAYERS AND THEIR CHARACTERISTICS

Mile Jedinak, Mark Milligan, and Tim Cahill

Mile Jedinak is a midfielder who signed with Aston Villa in 2016. He has a good shot from a distance, he takes free kicks well, he's a battler in the box, and he seems to take pleasure muscling others off the ball.

There's not much horsing around with Mark Milligan, who signed with Baniyas Club of Abu Dhabi in 2015. Essentially a defensive midfielder, from time to time, he can get forward with a strong shot from a distance. Though, he tends to sit back and play long balls from the central part of the field into the corner areas. When Australia needs a long throw-in, someone who can toss it all the way to the penalty kick area, he's their guy.

Tim Cahill is a veteran forward who has played with a variety of teams around the world, including England, the US, and China, and signed with Melbourne City FC in 2016. From his years of experience in the EPL, he gives Australia a guiding presence on the field, especially around the net. He's proficient scoring on crosses, he's got a good shot, he's accurate, he's passionate, and he's probably the best player Australia's produced.

KEY PLAYER STATS

	Games Played	Goals	Scoring Percentage
Mile Jedinak	73	18	24%
Mark Milligan	67	6	8%
Tim Cahill	104	50	48%

WHAT TO WATCH FOR ON TV—HOW MESSI, NEYMAR, KROOS, AND OTHERS PLAY

Australia wins the award for "embracing the new 'male bra' that many players are sporting these days." It's a black bra essentially, which is worn under the jersey, ostensibly to help an individual's performance. Not sure who won players over with this idea.

Australia will get in defensively, producing strong challenges and putting up a good fight. Offensively, they attempt a decent possession game, with lapses into long-ball soccer, which only gets them to another part of the field without much of a plan. Without any individual showmen, they'll produce a strong team effort, but getting goals will be difficult as they work their way through Russia, likely making an early exit.

Overall Team Rating: 6.8

IRAN

A BRIEF TEAM HISTORY

Iran's World Cup experience has not been very successful. From 1930-1974, they were not seen in a World Cup. Then, in 1978, they played but didn't make it past the first round. They withdrew in 1982. In 1986, they didn't compete in the World Cup. In 1990 and 1994, Iran didn't make it. In 1998, they finished slightly ahead of the United States, but didn't make it out of their group.

In 2002, they didn't make it. They made it to the 2006 World Cup, but didn't make it out of their group, finishing behind Portugal, Mexico, and Angola. They didn't make it to the 2010 World Cup in South Africa. While in Brazil 2014, Iran didn't get out of their group, which included Argentina, Nigeria, and Bosnia and Herzegovina.

On the way to Russia 2018, in the Asian Preliminary Competition, Iran finished first place in Group A, which consisted of South Korea (Korea Republic), Syria, Uzbekistan, China PR, and Qatar.

ASIAN COMPETITIONS

One of the better teams in Asia, Iran won the AFC Asian Cup in 1968, 1972, and 1976. They were champions of the Asian Games in 1974, 1990, and 1998; they won the West Asian Games in 1997; and they won the West Asian Championship in 2000, 2004, 2007, and 2008.

Sponsorship is always a fascinating facet of a team. Over the years, Iran has employed some mainstream brands and some other lessor known names to represent their team on the field. From 1978 on, they've entertained interesting looks from adidas, Amini, Shekari, Puma, Shekari (again), Daei Sport (an Iranian company founded by former player, Ali Daei), Puma, Merooj (an Iranian company founded by Dr. Majid Saedifar), Daei Sport (again), Legea, then, *voila!* They got Uhlsport (of all people), Givova (founded in Italy in 2008, don't ask), and back to adidas (as of 2016).

FACTS ABOUT THEIR COUNTRY

Iran, known in older days as Persia, has a population of approximately 82 million people, and a GDP of around 438 billion.

Javad Nekounam has the most caps for Iran with 151. Iran's leading goal-scorer is Ali Daei with 109. Currently, beer is not allowed in Iran, but some people watching might just be drinking non-alcoholic beer instead.

WHERE THE TEAM IS TODAY—TACTICS AND STRATEGIES

Should Iran win the World Cup in Russia, it would definitely make history. Any champion makes history, but in Iran's case, the footnote would read: "They pulled off a miracle." Like Australia, South Korea, Panama, Costa Rica, and a few others, the chances of Iran winning the whole thing are next to nothing. But they certainly have a good team, an ambitious one at that, and anything's possible.

Essentially, Iran employs a 4-3-3 formation which enables them to contest the ball defensively with greater aggression. Offensively, they're quick and play alluring balls into space for their teammates to gather. They tend to mix up the attack with a flurry of short passes combined with crosses into the box at a quick tempo. Long-winded, possession-oriented masters they are not.

CARLOS QUEIROZ—A BRIEF COACHING PORTRAIT

The coach is Carlos Queiroz, a former goalkeeper, born in Nampula, Portuguese Mozambique. He's coached a number of teams, including Portugal, the United Arab Emirates, South Africa, and Real Madrid. He began coaching Iran in 2011.

Under his direction, with the 4-3-3, the players are in great condition; Iran moves together as a unit, creating space, challenging for every loose ball, playing hard with a lot of effort, which creates a straightforward attack. Should they switch formations along the way to, say, a 4-4-2, things likely wouldn't change too much in their overall approach. They're not lulling defenders to sleep with slow possession play, that's for sure. They push the ball downfield, looking to get a telling pass into the box for quick scoring opportunities.

KEY PLAYERS AND THEIR CHARACTERISTICS

Ehsan Hajsafi, Masoud Shojaei, and Karim Ansarifard

Ehsan Hajsafi is a fast midfielder, typically found on the left side. He's got a strong shot from outside the box; he also has good accuracy with free kicks.

Masoud Shojaei is a very skillful, deceptive, and tricky dribbler in the midfield. He's often found on the ground because the other team has no option but to foul him.

Karim Ansarifard, who signed with Olympiacos in Greece in 2017, is a forward with good finishing instincts and awareness around the box. On top of that, he's a good passer, and Iran will look to use his talents for a strong run in the tournament.

KEY PLAYER STATS

	Games Played	Goals	Scoring Percentage
Ehsan Hajsafi	87	6	6%
Masoud Shojaei	70	8	11%
Karim Ansarifard	57	15	26%

WHAT TO WATCH FOR ON TV—HOW MESSI, NEYMAR, KROOS, AND OTHERS PLAY

Iran's instincts are to score goals. They go like sled dogs in the Arctic. When the whistle blows, the other team should expect a strong surge of energy from Iran. They push the ball up field with quickness, always searching for a chance to score. Should they get a lead, this might work against them a bit, as they don't seem to over-possess the ball very often. They're a team that goes full throttle with a lot of energy.

Overall Team Rating: 7

JAPAN

A BRIEF TEAM HISTORY

The first World Cup Japan entered was in 1998. They were knocked out in the group stage, ultimately finishing in 31st place.

As co-hosts in 2002, they made it to the second round. As for 2006, they were eliminated in the group stage. Then, in 2010, Japan made it to the second round again, only to be defeated by Paraguay. In 2014, they were again knocked out of the group stage.

On the way to Russia 2018, in the Asian Preliminary Competition, Japan finished first place in Group B, which consisted of Saudi Arabia, Australia, the United Arab Emirates, Iraq, and Thailand.

ASIAN COMPETITIONS

As for the AFC Asian Cup,* Japan currently leads all Asian competitors with four championships: 1992, 2000, 2004, and 2011.

---

* The AFC Asian Cup dates back to 1956. Behind Japan are Saudi Arabia and Iran, each with three titles, and South Korea with two.

FACTS ABOUT THEIR COUNTRY

Japan currently has an estimated population of 126 million people, and a GDP of about 5.1 trillion. National Foundation Day—which recognizes the first Japanese emperor, Emperor Jimmu—honors the year 660 BC and the founding of Japan.

The Japanese excel in many sports, including gymnastics and baseball, and they love their soccer. Japan's largest win came against the Philippines in 1967 by a score of 15-0. They showed them.

Kirin, Sapparo, and other beer brands will surely be on display in bars and house parties during Japan's games in Russia.

WHERE THE TEAM IS TODAY—TACTICS AND STRATEGIES

Japan's chances of winning the World Cup are low, but not completely off the chart. They're a middle-of-the-pack team with a high chance to do well and a low chance to actually walk away with the trophy for the first time.

Japan has gradually been making big strides in international soccer. The J League has been around for many years now, always a place for top-notch international talent—usually toward the end of their career or right before hitting rock bottom—and the result has been beneficial to the culture of Japanese soccer. The example of how to play the game correctly, as displayed by players like Jorginho and Zico, has been a great guide for a soccer-playing nation on the rise. This influence has transcended over to youth talent. And for those who reach the national team, only good things follow.

Japan will probably go with a 4-4-2. Defensively, they lack some confidence, but, they're every bit as talented as the other emerging teams around the world (such as the United States, Nigeria, and Iraq).

The Japanese style is very technically sound, with accurate passing, along with a thoughtful offensive buildup. If anything is holding them back, it's the overall belief that they belong at the top with traditional trendsetters like Brazil, Italy, and Germany.

VAHID HALILHODZIC—A BRIEF COACHING PORTRAIT

Vahid Halilhodzic is the current coach for Japan, having acquired the position in 2015. He was born in Yugoslavia and brings an interesting background as a player. From 1971-1987, he played for Velez (Bosnia and Herzegovina), Neretva (Croatia), Nantes (France), and Paris Saint-Germain (France) as a forward. He also played with the Yugoslavian national team from 1976-1985.

As a coach, he began in 1990, and since then he has led a variety of teams, including Velez, Lille, Paris Saint-Germain, Ittihad of Saudi Arabia, along with the national teams of Cote d'Ivoire and Algeria. His vast experience compliments Japan's ambitions well; it seems both parties are destined for big things, and they see Russia 2018 as their perfect platform.

Under Coach Vahid, Japan will play the 4-4-2 (unless drastic changes occur last minute), usually sitting back, very patient, allowing their opponent plenty of room into about the middle of their own defensive end (where they tend to amp up the pressure), while using their smart, pass-first approach in the attack.

KEY PLAYERS AND THEIR CHARACTERISTICS

Keisuke Honda, Shinji Okazaki, and Shinji Kagawa

Keisuke Honda—who has played with a few teams in the past, including CSKA Moscow and AC Milan—uses skill and perseverance on his quest to create havoc for goalies, which he does well, having scored over 35 goals for Japan since 2008. As of 2017, Honda began lending his talents to Pachuca in Mexico. Born in 1986, Honda is an established veteran and will have an impactful effect on the field for Japan.

Shinji Okazaki is a talented player and adept scorer, who was part of the successful Leicester City run in 2015 and 2016. As a forward, representing Japan since 2008, he has over 50 goals under his belt. He finishes accurately, even with some fancy guile every now and again.

Shinji Kagawa is an attacking midfielder with sublime touch and quick feet as if playing on a futsal court. He's played with Borussia Dortmund and Manchester United, as well as Cerezo Osaka in Japan. In all his stops, he's scored plenty of goals; over the past few years he's fine-tuned his passing in Europe, which will help Japan mount a serious attack on the old guard of soccer in Russia.

KEY PLAYER STATS

	Games Played	Goals	Scoring Percentage
Keisuke Honda	90	36	40%
Shinji Okazaki	108	50	46%
Shinji Kagawa	89	29	32%

WHAT TO WATCH FOR ON TV—HOW MESSI, NEYMAR, KROOS, AND OTHERS PLAY

As they continue to grow as a top-tier, soccer-playing nation, Japan resembles a touch of Spain meets Italy, steadily moving the ball through multiple channels with complete control as gifted attacking players wait up front, hoping to drive the ball into the back of the net. They're dangerous on the attack; their mental fortitude never quits. They're determined, driven, and convinced that sometime very soon they will win the World Cup.

In the coolest, most respectful way possible (if indeed it's possible), they subtly resemble a Japanese version of the bad boys from the Cobra Kai of *The Karate Kid*—Johnny, Bobby, and the rest—a cocky, self-aware group, sometimes dying their hair punk blonde for effect to show off their zest for life and self-assured arrogance. The cool thing about them, and for the future of Japanese soccer, is they know they're good. They have swagger. To them, it's only a matter of time before they conquer the World Cup.

What they lack in flashy individual speedsters soaring downfield, gliding past two or three defenders in full stride (like Kaka in his prime), they make up for with technical ability. They've got a little Iceman (from *Top Gun*, of course) in their veins. They wait, they wait…they're steady and they keep pushing forward, never giving up…and their patience usually keeps them in games.

Overall Team Rating: 7.9

Japan has a lot of work to do, but, currently, they have a good squad, deserving a 7.9.

SAUDI ARABIA

A BRIEF TEAM HISTORY

From 1930-1990, Saudi Arabia didn't make it to the World Cup. Finally arriving in 1994, they made the round of 16, but no farther. In 1998, 2002, and 2006, they were eliminated in the group phase. For 2010 and 2014, they failed to qualify.

Russia 2018 is their big return. On their way, Saudi Arabia finished second in Group B during the Asian Preliminary Competition. It was a tough group, consisting of Japan, Australia, the United Arab Emirates, Iraq, and Thailand, and that experience should serve them well at the World Cup.

ASIAN COMPETITIONS

For years, Saudi Arabia has been known throughout their extended region as one of the top teams. For the AFC Asian Cup, they've done quite well, winning it in 1984, 1988, and 1996. They have also taken first place in the Gulf Cup of Nations in 1994, 2002, and 2003. Furthermore, they've won the Arab Nations Cup in 1998 and 2002, while also earning the gold medal at the 2005 Islamic Solidarity Games.

FACTS ABOUT THEIR COUNTRY

Saudi Arabia, the land of oil and oasis, has a population of approximately 33 million people, and a GDP of around 689 billion.

Mohamed Al-Deayea has the most caps for Saudi Arabia with 178. Majed Abdullah, who played with Saudi Arabia from 1977-1994, has the most goals with 71. Practically all Saudi Arabian players also play on a Saudi club team. The country has a lot of pride for their soccer, and parties should be going all tournament long.

WHERE THE TEAM IS TODAY—TACTICS AND STRATEGIES

Saudi Arabia, a talented team, is searching for that breakthrough World Cup success. They're looking for a big year, which they're very capable of achieving. Of the teams with scant World Cup experience, they're among the favorites to go far in the tournament. With that said, their chances of winning the whole thing are very unlikely.

Playing in a 4-4-2, they might cough up a few defensive lapses from time to time, whether it's overcommitting and lunging on tackles, a clumsy decision in possession, or, instead of playing to the goalie, as a last resort, a defender might boom the ball downfield. If anything, the gaps in their defensive structure, which comes from lack of experience on a big stage, will be a major issue for them at World Cup Russia.

In the attack, they overlap frequently, getting players in motion on the wings, which creates passing options. However, like many teams, they lack in the department of two-man passing combinations, which leads to giveaways in traffic.

BERT VAN MARWIJK AND JUAN ANTONIO PIZZI—A BRIEF COACHING PORTRAIT

Bert van Marwijk was born in the Netherlands in 1952. He played as a midfielder with the Netherlands once in 1975. He has an impressive coaching résumé, including Borussia Dortmund and the Netherlands. He took over Saudi Arabia's team in 2015, which was a group full of talent.

Though, in 2017, Juan Antonio Pizzi stepped in as the Saudi Arabian coach. Pizzi brought his experience from coaching Chile. However, a change of coaching like this so soon before the World Cup brings with it an air of trepidation.

Saudi Arabia is a team waiting for their big moment. By waiting, they're literally knocking on the door of international soccer with solid team after solid team. Keeping the players motivated shouldn't be a problem. Rather, Pizzi simply needs to guide this super-talented, home-grown stash of players with confidence while keeping them within their game.

KEY PLAYERS AND THEIR CHARACTERISTICS

Yasser Al-Shahrani, Yahya Al-Shehri, and Mohammad Al-Sahlawi

Yasser Al-Shahrani is a younger defender looking to use his speed and athleticism to help keep opponents off the scoreboard.

Should he hypothetically transfer citizenship status over to Brazil, he's likely not someone that Coach Tite would call upon, but, as it stands, he's a good dribbler and an able attacking threat that provides a good spark for his team.

Yahya Al-Shehri is a quick midfielder who has the tendency to dribble across the goal box, looking for opportunities to score or pass. Add to that good lateral movement on the dribble and a tantalizing skill level with a few tricks up his sleeve. He's high on the list of current Saudi Arabian talent and part of a group that is expected to provide big results for their country.

Mohammad Al-Sahlawi is just a plain good finisher. Volleys, headers, running onto through-balls, accuracy around net...a real talent. He's scored many goals at the club level and for his country. Defenses should keep an eye on him.

KEY PLAYER STATS

	Games Played	Goals	Scoring Percentage
Yasser Al-Shahrani	24	0	0%
Yahya Al-Shehri	40	6	15%
Mohammad Al-Sahlawi	35	28	80%

WHAT TO WATCH FOR ON TV—HOW MESSI, NEYMAR, KROOS, AND OTHERS PLAY

Watch for a strong group that is in sync. Most of the players—if not all—exclusively play for Saudi Arabian club teams. So they know each other very well.

They're like the Netherlands meets Brazil of the Middle East, minus the international track record. In midfield and up front, they have smooth ball-handlers that intertwine fluid passing from wing to wing. They're fun to watch, and the players are very confident. Though, what sets Brazil apart from most teams is their extremely confident and competent defenders who add so much to the attacking side of the game, whereas the Saudi Arabian defenders are not quite at the Brazilian level. The Saudis have so much talent, but lack a little ingenuity from their defensive players. Aside from that, they have the capability to make huge strides all tournament long.

Overall Team Rating: 7.2

SOUTH KOREA

A BRIEF TEAM HISTORY

South Korea didn't play in the 1930, 1934, 1938, or 1950 World Cups. In 1954, they were eliminated in the group stage, leaving Switzerland early. They didn't compete in 1958, 1962, 1966, 1970, 1974, 1978, or 1982. South Korea had their chance in 1986. Unfortunately, they were better known for clobbering Maradona with cheap shots and career-ending tackles than anything else. And, for 1990, 1994, and 1998, they were eliminated in the group stage. To that point, they were merely a decent sparring partner.

Then came destiny. Prior to the 2014 World Cup, South Korea was the first—and only—Asian team to make the semifinals of a World Cup. They did it in 2002 with a phenomenal side (some say an excessively rough side that bumped hard and took no prisoners*), including Seol Ki-hyeon, Park Ji-sung, Kim Nam-il, Yoo Sang-chul, and Ahn Jung-hwan, coached by the traveling Dutch coach and "football genius," Guus Hiddink.

---

* Over the years, as they've progressed technically and tactically, they've never lacked commitment, effort, or physical play. In other words, they may possess a nonconfrontational façade, but they don't joke around.

As co-hosts, each game was filled with Korean fans who chanted in unison continuously throughout each game like some grand orchestra, thousands strong. It was an amazing spectacle, and in three games, in the eleventh hour, when they needed a goal to survive, it arrived, setting the throng of supporters to vocal ecstasy. By the time they met Germany in the semifinals, they had run out of steam, eventually placing fourth overall.

By the looks of their progress, and that of Japan, it wouldn't be a surprise to see more Asian teams going to the semifinals again very soon. However, on paper, their progress has gone back to the South Korea of old. By 2006, they were eliminated in the group stage. In 2010, they improved to the round of 16, but no farther. And, in 2014, they couldn't get past the group stage.

Yet, they remain a quality team, bound by the unwritten—and sometimes less understood—contract of the modern World Cup which essentially says: The competition has leveled out so much that even traditional powers like Italy (2010, 2014) and England (2014) might not get out of their group.

On the way to Russia 2018, South Korea finished second in their Asian Preliminary Competition group. As one of Asia's most consistent programs, South Korea is looking to do well in the 2018 World Cup and beyond.

ASIAN COMPETITIONS

South Korea has a big presence on the Asian soccer scene, winning the AFC Asian Cup in 1956 and 1960, while earning second and third place a number of times. They've done well at the EAFF East Asian Cup, winning in 2003, 2008, and 2015.

At the Asian Games, they took first place in 1970, 1978, 1986, and 2014.

FACTS ABOUT THEIR COUNTRY

South Korea's population is around 50 million people, and their GDP is approximately 1.4 trillion. They're a global leader in many areas, including the manufacturing of automobiles and the technology field. Known also for great food and ancient culture, South Koreans love their soccer, and their natural soccer rival is their close neighbor, Japan.

Hong Myung-bo (1990-2002), who played 38 games with the LA Galaxy from 2003-2004, has the most South Korean caps with 136.

Hite is a beer often enjoyed by South Koreans, and it will probably be passed around en masse as people hover around TV sets during the games in Russia.

WHERE THE TEAM IS TODAY—TACTICS AND STRATEGIES

South Korea's chances of winning the World Cup are not too good. However, they're a middle-of-the-pack team. Anything's possible. There's a much higher chance of them winning than a few other teams with less World Cup experience, but they're definitely not a favorite.

They play with subdued passion. In their culture, there's a strong emphasis on respecting elders. In some cases, elders cannot be challenged. This was something coach Hiddink had to grapple with (in regard to team chemistry) during the 2002 World Cup adventure, and when he got everybody on the same page, they did quite well. In fact, they reached the semifinals. Should the current South Korean team get on board with what the 2002 team had going on, good things might be around the corner.

Their formation is typically that of a 4-3-3, with players checking in and out frequently. Defensively, they collapse quickly on the ball in small groups. They use their bodies well, often looking for contact. Offensively, they check in and out, receiving the ball and distributing it from wing to wing, often switching play with a long ball. Areas they could improve include patience in possession, which would lessen their attempts to hasten attacking passes toward goal. Their team lacks individual ingenuity—the ability for a few individuals to go at players and take over the game. This will be their downfall for Russia 2018, and World Cups in the near future, unless they make drastic changes.

ULI STIELIKE—A BRIEF COACHING PORTRAIT

Uli Stielike took the coaching job in South Korea in 2014. Previously, he played with West Germany from 1975-1984 as a midfielder and defender. He also played with Real Madrid in the 70s and 80s. Under his direction, the team is playing an upbeat style, stifling their opponents with tough, aggressive defense, while pushing the attack and forcing the issue.

KEY PLAYERS AND THEIR CHARACTERISTICS

Hong Jeong-ho, Koo Ja-cheol, and Kim Shin-wook

Hong Jeong-ho is a solid, dependable defender who South Korea is leaning on for guidance on the backline.

Koo Ja-cheol is a utilitarian midfielder with experience at FC Augsburg in Germany.

Kim Shin-wook, or "Wookie" as he's called from here on out, is a tall forward, around 6'5", who uses his body well in the box. He's a head-ball specialist, a little like the South Korean version of Niall Quinn.

KEY PLAYER STATS

	Games Played	Goals	Scoring Percentage
Hong Jeong-ho	41	2	4%
Koo Ja-cheol	63	18	28%
Kim Shin-wook	38	3	7%

WHAT TO WATCH FOR ON TV—HOW MESSI, NEYMAR, KROOS, AND OTHERS PLAY

South Korea will give a strong effort, with tough tackles, aggressive play, and upbeat passing as they develop a quick, dynamic attack. Their players aren't flamboyant dribblers; rather, they play a solid team game, getting everyone involved and relying on fluid movement from players in overlapping positions.

Will they need the help of 4,320 offside calls in their favor to win the whole thing? Possibly not that much help, but they'll definitely require some lucky breaks to become champions in Russia.

Overall Team Rating: 7.8

OCEANIA (1/2)

The teams of Oceania received "half a berth" of a chance for World Cup 2018, so says the FIFA website. This means the teams of Oceania have qualification rounds—or "Preliminary Competition," as FIFA calls it—just like the rest of the world. But, only one team from Oceania gets a playoff with the fifth-place team of South America.

At the close of 2017, New Zealand qualified to a playoff with the South American representative, Peru. It took place in November of 2017.* Peru ended up winning the two-game playoff (the first game was 0-0 and in the second Peru won 2-0), and New Zealand lost their chance to attend the World Cup. So, as a result, Oceania didn't qualify a team for World Cup Russia. Better luck next time.

---

* The games were held on November 11, 2017, in New Zealand, and November 15, 2017, in Peru.

Those are the 32 teams of the 2018 World Cup. They are the lucky few. For some teams, it may seem like it will take an Egyptian Great Year of 25,920 years to win the World Cup. Or a great upset could occur at any time. Many teams listed could be that upset team. While many of these teams will likely *not* win the whole thing, their presence as lower-ranked teams with the potential to pull off something spectacular is just a part of what makes the World Cup interesting. Every game has a place. And every team contributes to the excitement.

CHAPTER 2

WORLD CUP HISTORY

A BRIEF OVERVIEW OF EACH WORLD CUP FROM 1930 TO TODAY

THE WINNERS AND FUN FACTS

Many nations have tried and failed. They've gone for that trophy, that elusive trophy. For all we know, there's only one champion in the entire universe. Should there be life out there, the chances of them playing soccer right down to the exact rules and specifications that we do is pretty doubtful. So for now, the World Cup champions remain champions of the world and the universe. That's the allure of the World Cup.

In the long, illustrious, history of the grand tournament, only a few nations have really come out on top. As the leader in World Cup championship game appearances with eight,* Germany has made an unprecedented claim to being one of the top three countries to ever field a team. It's hard to get to the finals. For one, everyone has to go through Germany, Brazil, and Italy to get there. Following them are teams like Argentina, France, England, and Uruguay, to name a few. The whole world tries, but when it comes down to it, only a few nations have had much luck getting past the semifinals.

Teams that have reached the finals of the illustrious World Cup are: Germany, Brazil, Italy, Argentina, Uruguay, France, England, Spain, the Netherlands, Czech Republic, Hungary, and Sweden.

---

* As of 2014, Brazil was second with a total of seven World Cup championship game appearances.

And that's it. Germany and Brazil have led the group for years. The actual champions, the owners of the World Cup, include Brazil (5), Germany (4), Italy (4), Argentina (2), Uruguay (2), Spain (1), France (1), and England (1). A few other teams that showed promise early on have drifted in and out of relevance. For instance, everything after 1960 has not been that good for Uruguay, Hungary, or the Czech Republic.

Uruguay has two titles from 1930 and 1950. Since 1950, they've fallen off. However, they remain competitive, but something in their game is predictably boring. Similarly, Hungary and the Czech Republic had second place finishes during the same twenty-year era, and, subsequently, they lost their place among the elite.

England found their way to the final once and has had a difficult run ever since. Yet, should they qualify, teams like England, Uruguay, the Czech Republic, and Sweden have been competitive threats in the World Cup, often acting as buffers in the early rounds, always hoping for something better.

In practically every sense of the word, the World Cup is cyclical. Soccer programs ebb and flow, new players come and go, new stories emerge, new drama awaits, and every four years—which may seem like an eternity, but it's just the right amount of time for everyone around the globe to recharge their batteries—billions of people get revved up for it all over again. Before you know it, qualifications have wrapped up, and the world comes together for the big tournament.

Amid all the new stadiums and big salaries, it's easy to forget the first gathering back in 1930. Under the guidance of coach

Alberto Suppici, Uruguay hosted and took the trophy. They wore the gawky, baggy, almost whimsical shorts. Compared to today's equipment, the shoes and ball looked quite a bit different as well. For starters, pretty much everyone had the same style shoe: black, with no design. Unless you consider shoelaces a design. Today's players have all kinds of different shoes made by companies like adidas, Puma, and Nike, featuring different colors ranging from black, white, purple, blue, green, orange, yellow, and many fluorescent combinations in between. It's a far cry from the 1930s shoe version of the Ford Model T. And the ball back in 1930 looked more like a volleyball someone picked up last minute from a local gymnasium.

Some of the older games—viewable on VHS, DVD, and YouTube—might also come across as archaic. They were filmed in black and white, and the players appear to be waddling around.

As the years have gone by, the shoes and ball have progressed in appearance and technical ability, and for each World Cup, something new is around the corner. Yet, everything started in a distant time.

By the time Italy won consecutive titles in 1934 (hosted by Italy) and 1938 (hosted by France), the United States was in the Great Depression. Italy's coach for the two titles was Vittorio Pozzo. Then World War II arrived, and the World Cup was postponed.

As the war ended in 1945, things got rolling again in 1950, as Uruguay became champions for the second time, defeating Brazil in a famous game at the Maracana Stadium in Rio de Janeiro in front of approximately 200,000 spectators—some say more. Uruguay's coach was Juan Lopez.

Four years later, the games were held in scenic Switzerland. West Germany—with help from Werner Liebrich and Helmut Rahn (aka "the Boss")—got their first title in 1954, defeating Hungary in the final. Germany's coach at the helm was Sepp Herberger.

Then, the game changed a bit as Brazil ushered in a new era with the emerging talent of Pele and Garrincha. It was the 1958 World Cup hosted by Sweden. Brazil's first World Cup champion coach was Vicente Feola. His decision to play Pele and Garrincha set Brazil in a new direction. The game was already starting to creep toward higher quality and style, but things really picked up from there.

The 1960s, so it is said, belonged to Pele, the "king of soccer." He and his Brazilian teammates incorporated a lot of creative flair and skill, which still trickles over to this day.

In the World Cup of 1962—down in beautiful Chile—Pele was injured for most of the tournament, though Brazil repeated as champions with Garrincha leading the way. His center stage performance, including remarkable dribbling skills and numerous goals, had a great impact, making the argument that he was one of the greatest players of all time. Brazil's coach was Aymore Moreira.

GREAT WORLD CUP MOMENT

"Garrincha came inside, not on the wing, came inside and he turned around as though he was going to pass the ball, and instead, just bent the ball right into the top corner. There again, somewhere else he shouldn't have been. But, sensational, sensational skill." Bobby Charlton reflecting on Garrincha's goal against England in the 1962 World Cup quarterfinal.

England, featuring the talent of Bobby Charlton, Geoff Hurst, and many others, finally won the World Cup in 1966, coincidentally, the same year they hosted. Since then, don't ask...unless you're ready for a long dissertation of near misses, including but not limited to the "hand of God," poor referee decisions, and overwhelming disappointment. For the big run in 1966, England's coach was Alf Ramsey.

Pele—along with Rivellino, Jairzinho, and others—earned Brazil a third title in 1970, the famous World Cup hosted in Mexico. It was televised in color (for many television sets) around the world. Brazil's coach was Mario Zagallo, who was also a player for Brazil's first two titles in 1958 and 1962.

West Germany—led by Gerd Müller and Franz Beckenbauer—won their second title in 1974 when they hosted the tournament for the first time. West Germany's coach for this historic event was Helmut Schön.

Argentina, wearing the white and blue stripes, won their first title in 1978 on a field littered with confetti when they played host for the first time. Were there allegations of corruption at the tournament? Yes. Brazil, Argentina, Peru, and Poland were in a second-round group to decide who would go onto the championship game.* People from the Brazilian camp accused the Argentineans of manipulating the referees and Peruvian players for the Peru and Argentina game, which leaned heavily in Argentina's favor—6-0. As a result, Argentina moved on to play the Netherlands in the final. For their first World Cup title, Argentina's coach was Cesar Luis Menotti.

Spain hosted in 1982, showcasing the beautiful cities of Madrid, Barcelona, Sevilla, Bilbao, Valladolid, Malaga, Valencia, Zaragoza, Elche, Oviedo, Gijon, Alicante, Vigo, and A Coruna. Italy, ushering in the magical decade of the 80s, won their third title, tying Brazil for most championships of all time. Their coach for this great adventure was Enzo Bearzot.

In 1986, Mexico hosted for the second time, with games played in Mexico City, Guadalajara, Puebla, Monterrey, Queretaro City, Leon, Nezahualcoyotl, Irapuato, Zapopan, and Toluca. Argentina won their second title with a great individual performance from Maradona, setting the wheels in motion in his favor as the best player of all time. Argentina's coach was Carlos Bilardo.

---

* The format in 1978 was different than today's World Cup. There was an original group stage of four groups (with four teams in each group). From that, the top two teams of each group moved onto the final group stage (the "second round"), which consisted of two groups (with four teams in each group). From that, the first-place team of each group met in the final game.

GREAT WORLD CUP MOMENT

"Maradona turns like a little eel, and comes away from trouble, little squat man. Comes inside Butcher, leaves him for dead, outside Bennett, leaves him for dead, and puts the ball away, and that is why Maradona is the greatest player in the world!" An English commentator during Maradona's "Goal of the Century" in the quarterfinal against England, World Cup 1986.

Italy was host in 1990, featuring games played in Rome, Milan, Naples, Turin, Bari, Verona, Florence, Cagliari, Bologna, Udine, Palermo, and Genoa. Guided by the midfield play of Lothar Matthäus, West Germany walked away with authority as champions, making it their third title. The coach was the great Franz Beckenbauer, who was a player on the 1974 championship team. Also, it was the last tournament they would compete in as West Germany; from then on, they were unified again as Germany.

The United States hosted for the first time in 1994, providing venues in New York, Boston, Washington, DC, Orlando, Dallas, Detroit, Chicago, San Francisco, and Los Angeles. Brazil—with the help of Romario, Bebeto, and Dunga—won their fourth title, defeating Italy in the final by way of penalty kicks. This made Brazil the first team to reach four titles. (Italy and Germany each had three.) Their coach for this huge accomplishment was Carlos Alberto Parreira.

In the 1998 World Cup, hosted by France, games were held in Saint-Denis, Paris, Marseille, Lyon, Lens, Nantes, Toulouse,

FUN FACTS

The United States leads all World Cup hosts in total attendance for all games: 3,587,538 people.[12] Brazil 2014 comes in second, with a total attendance of 3,429,873.[13] There was another figure of Brazil's total attendance from 2014, also from FIFA's website, oddly enough. It is 3,386,810.[14] As for average attendance per game: United States 1994 is out in front with 68,991, Brazil 2014 comes in second with over 52,000,* and Germany 2006 comes in third with 52,491.†

* It turns out, there are three different figures for the 2014 World Cup Brazil average attendance per game. The main source of information seems to be FIFA, and, possibly, over time, the actual attendance numbers they gathered may have changed due to new information.

According to FIFA.com, "2014 FIFA World Cup Brazil in numbers," the Brazil 2014 average attendance figure was 53,592. However, according to FIFA.com, "FIFA World Cup All Time Statistics," the Brazil 2014 average attendance figure was 52,918.

At Reuters, from an article featured online, "Average World Cup attendance is second highest ever," by Mike Collett, from July 6, 2014, the Brazil 2014 average attendance figure was 52,762. These figures were accessed June 17, 2017.

† Both FIFA.com and Reuters listed Germany 2006 at 52,491. This figure was accessed June 17, 2017.

Saint-Etienne, Bordeaux, and Montpellier. Zidane led the way, as France won their first World Cup title, defeating Brazil in the final before a packed house in Paris. Aime Jacquet was the coach guiding the way.

The 2002 World Cup, shared by South Korea and Japan, was a unique event. It was hosted in cities spread out across South Korea (Seoul, Daegu, Busan, Incheon, Ulsan, Suwon, Gwangju, Jeonju, Daejeon, Jeju) and Japan (Yokohama, Saitama, Shizuoka, Osaka, Miyagi, Oita, Niigata, Ibaraki, Kobe, Sapporo). Brazil gained their fifth title, defeating Germany 2-0 in the final. Five titles put Brazil out in front of all nations as the undisputed champs...the leaders of the game. Their coach was Luiz Felipe Scolari.

Germany took up hosting the Cup in 2006, showing off state-of-the-art arenas and featuring games in Berlin, Dortmund, Munich, Stuttgart, Gelsenkirchen, Hamburg, Frankfurt, Cologne, Hanover, Leipzig, Kaiserslautern, and Nuremberg. With a unified team, Italy emerged as champions, making it their fourth title. Marcello Lippi was the Italian coach.

World Cup 2010, hosted for the first time in Africa, landed in South Africa, featuring games played in Johannesburg, Cape Town, Durban, Pretoria, Port Elizabeth, Rustenburg, Polokwane, Nelspruit, and Bloemfontein. For the first time in their history, Spain won the World Cup thanks to a late goal from Iniesta, beating the Netherlands in the final. It was an interesting championship game, in that, no matter what, there was going to be a new champion as Spain and the Netherlands had never won a World Cup before. Vicente del Bosque led the team as coach.

In 2014, Brazil, the best team in World Cup history, hosted for the second time.* Games were played across the large geographic landscape in Rio de Janeiro, Sao Paolo, Brasilia, Fortaleza, Belo

---

* The first time was in 1950.

FUN FACTS

A round trip vacation to the southern tip of Africa cost a minimum amount of $30,000. The Vuvuzelas—the "annoying" horns that echoed throughout the games— weren't as popular as people thought they might be. In fact, there were efforts (albeit, fruitless) to have them banned from stadiums.

Horizonte, Porto Alegre, Salvador, Recife, Cuiaba, Manaus, Natal, and Curitiba.

Brazil just couldn't catch a break as hosts. They lost the heartbreaker to Uruguay in 1950, and, in 2014, they took a tough defeat from Germany in the semifinals by a score of 7-1. Germany, with a great team, including Klose, Kroos, Özil, and Neuer, walked away with the title for the fourth time in their history. This achievement tied them with Italy, both teams one title behind Brazil. Their coach was the calm and thoughtful Joachim Löw.

THE 2014 DOPING PREVENTION

Working with FIFA, the Swiss Laboratory for Doping Analyses[16] conducted drug tests for players before the 2014 tournament. Apparently, about 91% of players were actually tested. Then, for each game, FIFA and the Doping Analyses team would test two players from each team, according to FIFA.com, from June 17, 2014. FIFA was criticized by some—such as *The Irish Times*[17]—for the testing methods put forth. Critics felt more could have been done to eradicate any possible use of performance-enhancing drugs (PEDs).

FUN FACTS

FIFA.com[15] listed a few interesting details from the 2014 World Cup in Brazil:

- 16,746 printed media accreditations were produced during this World Cup.
- There were 3,127,674 food and beverage transactions that took place at the stadiums during the competition.
- During the 267-day FIFA World Cup Trophy Tour by Coco-Cola, 90 countries were visited, and the trophy was touch by 45 heads of state and 33 previous World Cup winners, among others.
- FIFA's Global Stadium, FIFA.com's social, online, and mobile hub saw a more than one billion overall attendance throughout Brazil 2014, equating to 13,380 sold-out Maracanas.
- Also, quite a few adidas balls were used. As reported on FIFA.com, 3,240 balls were used as for training and matches.
- Throughout the 2014 World Cup, the teams traveled by plane a lot, almost the equivalent of seven laps around the world, according to FIFA.com.
- In terms of goals, FIFA.com reports that 171 goals, an average of 2.67 per game, tied Brazil 2014 as the highest-scoring World Cup of all time, level with the 1998 World Cup in France.

THE LEADING SCORERS FROM EACH WORLD CUP

Cup Year	Player (Country)	Number of Goals
1930	Guillermo Stabile (Argentina)	8
1934	Oldrich Nejedly (Czechoslovakia)	5
1938	Leonidas (Brazil)	7
1950	Ademir (Brazil)	8
1954	Sandor Kocsis (Hungary)	11
1958	Just Fontaine (France)	3
1962	Florian Albert (Hungary), Valentin Ivanov (Soviet Union), Garrincha (Brazil), Vava (Brazil), Drazan Jerkovic (Yugoslavia), Leonel Sanchez (Chile)	4
1966	Eusebio (Portugal)	9
1970	Gerd Müller (West Germany)	10
1974	Grzegorz Lato (Poland)	7
1978	Mario Kempes (Argentina)	6
1982	Paolo Rossi (Italy)	6
1986	Gary Lineker (England)	6

(continued)

The Leading Scorers From Each World Cup *(continued)*

1990	Salvatore Schillaci (Italy)	6
1994	Oleg Salenko (Russia), Hristo Stoichkov (Bulgaria)	6
1998	Davor Suker (Croatia)	6
2002	Ronaldo (Brazil)	8
2006	Miroslav Klose (Germany)	5
2010	Thomas Müller (Germany)	5
2014	James Rodriguez (Colombia)	6

THE TOP 5 SCORERS IN WORLD CUP HISTORY

1. Miroslav Klose (Germany)	16
2. Ronaldo (Brazil)	15
3. Gerd Müller (West Germany)	14
4. Just Fontaine (France)	13
5. Pele (Brazil)	12

THE INTERESTING ROLE OF CORNER KICKS IN THE WORLD CUP

A LOOK AT PAST CORNER KICK SUCCESS AND WHAT TO EXPECT IN RUSSIA

The persisting obsession with venerating the almighty corner kick lurks around the world. A *Bloomberg* article online presents an attempt at understanding possibly the most overrated moment in soccer: the corner kick. It says: "Corner kicks in the World Cup are valuable opportunities for attacking teams to score. From where to aim to how to curve the ball, we asked a professional player from the New York Red Bulls for a step-by-step guide on how to take the ultimate corner kick."[18] The ultimate corner kick? Sometimes, the corner kick is revered way too much.

From the movie, *Victory*, Michael Caine, Pele, and a group of ragtime former professional players stuck in a German POW camp in the middle of World War II didn't know what to make of their newly found American goalie. Of course, Hatch, played by Sylvester Stallone, asked the famous question, "Where do I stand for a corner kick?" Good old Hatch. He couldn't pass, he couldn't dribble, but he was a good goalkeeper.

An Englishman might pull you aside and explain how vital a corner kick is and how important a good cross is. And, in regard to technically crossing the ball, it is important to have good "service," but concentrating too much on these fastidious issues ignores the avenues that get a team into scoring positions, which would be creative ballhandling with sound structure in possession or moving across the field, as opposed to always forcing the ball down the line. Nevertheless, it's easy to rely on crosses and corners as an opportunistic avenue to make an impact on the game.

Are corners a complete a waste of time? Yes, and no. Sure, they serve an occasional purpose. Goals show up sometimes, of course. No one should be completely unrealistic about the place and purpose of the corner kick.

Interestingly, evidence has shown how hard it is to score on corners.

On July 24, 2016, Sporting KC of the MLS went past 100 corners with zero success. This is common for teams around the world. It's just plain hard to score on a corner. When a goal does happen, say, during a World Cup, all the world's attention goes to the score, seeing it as normal, disregarding all the times it doesn't happen.

Speaking of the 2014 World Cup, according to Michael Caley of *The Washington Post*, on June 24, 2014: "There have been sixteen goals scored off 358 corners, compared with an expected tally of 10 or 11 goals from that many corner kicks."[19] Whether it's 16 goals, 10 or 11, it's still out of 358. The final say is: Corners are difficult to score on.

Thanks to huge moments, like Italy tying the game with France from a corner kick in the final of the 2006 World Cup, it seems as if they are handy tools in the game. And they can be, as long as people live in a world of reality while understanding the waste of time corners ultimately represent.

There is an overemphasis around the world from multiple teams over the importance of corners, which is simply the cross's uneducated second cousin. To say corners are more important than possession play is like the guy who says things like, "You know the truth of the matter is quite simple: Lab monkeys have been secretly ruling the world this whole time." The corner kick is definitely no Rhode's Scholar, nor are the people propagating its relevance in the larger scheme of things. Too many teams prolong this superfluous addiction to "winning a corner," as most enthusiasts say. And though corners are important, in the grand scheme of things, as the facts show, they're fool's gold.

Insofar as corners *not being a waste of time*: It's been suggested that inward swerving crosses to the near post will yield more goals than any other kind, as shown in research data from analysts who watched countless corner kicks which inevitably brought them to that assessment. The study that concluded this was funded by Manchester City. The almighty Manchester City—with funds reaching into the billions of dollars, under the ownership of City Football Group (part of Abu Dhabi United Group), yeah, that Manchester City—decided they were going to crack the code of corners, which ostensibly they did.

That's great, go with it. But the teams that understand that corners are essentially a waste of time will be better off focusing their utmost attention on the fastidious details that pertain to possession and other tactical matters in the flow of play. Caveman says, "Possession give more success." How did the Golden Generation of Spain often deal with a corner being "awarded" to them? They'd typically play the ball short and begin the passing sequences all over again. Hint to teams on the bubble: Barbaric corners have a place unless possession can override them.

History has shown that for any team to get excited over corners, and only corners, means they're barking up the wrong tree. The overall approach for a successful World Cup team should involve getting more excited over creative play that leads to corners, not the corners in and of themselves.

As the World Cup knows: To score on a corner is grand, like West Germany tying Argentina in the championship of 1986 on two consecutive goals from corners. How dramatic it was! But, all in all, they're extremely hard to stumble upon. Essentially, 10-16 goals out of 358 tries. Imagine that.

TOP FLOPPING TEAMS

THE INFAMOUS FLOP IS EXPLAINED

First off, the best flop from past World Cups would likely have to be the notorious Rivaldo flop near the corner flag in the 2002 World Cup. As flops go, if he were a singer, his name would have to be The Big Bopper.

Another famous example, coincidentally from Brazil (or is it?), would be the 1986 World Cup quarterfinal match in which Socrates and his crew—including Junior and Careca—were up against Platini, Giresse, Tigana, and the elegant French. This particular case, in fairness, borders on flopping by way of flopping skills put to use. Branco went down in the French penalty box and rolled around searching for the pain. Was he fouled, or wasn't he? It was hard to tell in real time, though it definitely looked like a foul. However, some flopping know-how (which we'll cover momentarily) was definitely added to ensure a penalty. When the foul was awarded, he raised his arms in victory. Then Zico missed the penalty kick.

In general, flopping has been regarded by many as, (1) a keen way of getting the referee to call fouls on your behalf, (2) a clever way to waste time near the end of a game to ensure a victory, and, (3) a complete nuisance.

If anything positive can be said about the flopping strategy, it's this: The main intent is to get the referee to call a foul immediately and to work the referee so that he calls more fouls later in the game. However, many people argue it's just a waste of time. Is it strategy? Is it calling out for help on a deeper level than just a foul? The flop is intriguing on many levels. For those new to the flop, it can be described in the following ways.

Scenario One: A typical flop is when a player is not fouled at all but desperately wants to fool the referee into thinking a foul has occurred. So they fake a foul, along with a fake injury that was caused by the fake foul. Basically, there's a lot of fakery going on. This includes rolling on the ground, writhing in pain, moaning, wincing, grabbing the legs, and calling for the medical staff, along with the stretcher, along with a priest to administer last rites. "Oh, my ankle! Oh, dear God, the agony! *Oh, the agony*! Maybe my $20 million contract will be able to afford a pair of crutches for all the pain I'm enduring!" Sometimes referees can be fooled. "Is he really hurt? Was that really a foul? What am I not seeing out here?" This is what the flopper wants the referee to think. It's an ongoing game of acting. And the referee has to be on high alert for such a thing.

Scenario Two: A player gets slightly fouled and embellishes the affair by rolling around on the ground, accompanied by the usual shenanigans: grimacing and writhing in pain and what not, hoping the referee gives a yellow card.

Scenario Three: There are times, in fact, when a real foul occurs, a kick to the leg for instance, which may in fact hurt, and the injured player uses flopping know-how to get the point across to the referee that a yellow card should be shown. So, in fact, in this case, it wouldn't be a flop. However, sometimes it's hard for the referee to see the foul committed, and, based on past flopping, the whole "don't cry wolf" element is being considered. Not wanting to be fooled, the referee is conflicted based on all past flopping activity, trickery, and apropos shenanigans. So therefore, previous floppers of the Scenario One persuasion can be blamed for the referee not being sympathetic when a real foul occurs. The usual outcome: The cards stay in the pocket. The moral to the story: Flopping doesn't pay. A few teams that might lead the flopping category: Serbia, Argentina, Brazil, Portugal, Mexico, Nigeria, Croatia, Saudi Arabia, Colombia, and Uruguay.

CHAPTER 3

FIFA: THE ORGANIZING BODY OF WORLD CUPS

SOME BACKGROUND INFORMATION ON FIFA

The organizing body behind world soccer is FIFA. Originally, their first office was established in Paris in 1904. Their base has since moved to Zurich, Switzerland. FIFA organizes plenty of other soccer-related events, and they even have a popular videogame named after them. However, their biggest event would be the men's World Cup. And when it comes to the allocation of World Cups, and practically everything that goes along with it, they're in charge.

Throughout all past World Cups, FIFA has organized each tournament with a hand in all the decision-making, including the choice of host nation, rules and regulations, referee appointments, stadium construction, sponsorship, and as you'll see, much more…

FIFA HEADQUARTERS

All committee meetings or daily business conducted at the headquarters takes place inside the beautiful, modern, voyeuristic-style building that is the main office. The outside is presented as *rectangular*, assembling what appears to be a cube shape. The FIFA emblem, which looks like it's polished twice daily, resides by the front door implanted into a gray brick wall, and it shines with a pristine, silver-mirror finish, reflecting the lush, grassy, well-kept lawn and trees surrounding the property. By night, the whole outer perimeter can glow a hue of blue and violet, looking like something from another planet, maybe Neptune, or a distant make-believe planet that a Daft Punk video would be shot on. It's the kind of work office that makes vacation look like a bad idea.

Inside are elegant halls and rooms with shiny, waxed floors made from some kind of marble that God must have personally selected. The inner chambers provide an ideal setting for entertaining a variety of invited guests, ranging from heads of state to well-known players such as David Beckham. Within the halls of FIFA is the famous "war room" as it's called, which is, by now, universally accepted as the equivalent to the meeting quarters in *Dr. Strangelove*; it's a large, imposing room, where FIFA leaders meet to discuss world soccer matters. It's reflective of the grand vision FIFA has set in motion: to bring soccer to every corner of the globe.

FIFA MEMBERSHIP

From around the world, there are many soccer-playing nations that are members of FIFA. And each one is part of a continental confederation (such as CONCACAF, UEFA, and so on). In the modern era, they have separated world soccer into six confederations: CONMEBOL (South America), CONCACAF (North America), UEFA[20] (Europe), CAF (Africa), AFC (Asia), and OFC (Oceania).

Any soccer-playing nation has the potential to be a member of FIFA. The general scope looks like this:

* Europe: 53 members[21]
* Asia: 46 members
* Oceania: 11 members

- Africa: 54 members
- North America: 41 members[22]
- South America: 10 members

RANKINGS AND AWARDS

Some of the many tasks within FIFA include ranking teams and awarding players with top honors. Teams that are part of FIFA are subjected to the FIFA World rankings which are updated monthly, ordering each team based on their performance in international competition, qualifiers, and friendlies.

Each year, the best player in the world is announced under the title "FIFA Ballon d'Or." Prior to 2009, it was called the "FIFA Player of the Year," which merged with the "Ballon d'Or" in 2010.

LAWS OF THE GAME

Probably felt as a sigh of relief by most Committee Members, the laws that govern soccer, known officially as the "Laws of the Game," are not solely the responsibility of FIFA. These laws are also maintained by the International Football Association Board (known as IFAB). FIFA has four members on IFAB, and the other four members are provided by the football associations of England, Scotland, Wales, and Northern Ireland, who originally established IFAB in 1882. The English are recognized for the creation of the game and have held on to this point of honor, wherein, to this day, any changes to the "Laws of the Game" must be agreed on by at least six of the eight members (of IFAB).

FIFA has the right to suspend teams or lay down some sort of sanction, which may, from time to time, conflict with the views of the founders of the game, who, in the opinion of many fans around the world, sit around in fancy offices wasting a lot of time and money going over superfluous details.

Any wrangling between FIFA and IFAB dates back to the inception of FIFA in 1904 by a group of Frenchmen, who, as portrayed in the film *United Passions*, were fed up with the British controlling everything. *United Passions*—a movie that comes across as an in-house production by FIFA, said by some to be in league with the "worst films ever made,"[23] starring Tim Roth* and Gerard Depardieu—drove this point home in the beginning of the film with great authority. Still, as the organizing body of world soccer, FIFA has a system in place to keep the game in order.

The governing system of FIFA consists of four general bodies: the Congress, the Executive Committee, the General Secretariat, along with Standing and Ad-hoc Committees. These four branches are meant to keep appropriate *checks and balances in place*. Critics have said that there needs to be more transparency at FIFA, and the checks and balances are way out of whack. Criticism turned into reality and took the world by storm in 2015.

TROUBLE IN PARADISE: FIFA MAKES WORLDWIDE NEWS

On May 27, 2015, it was announced that multiple high-ranking members of FIFA were arrested.

---

* Roth distanced himself from the film with criticism.

Chuck Blazer, an American citizen and a leader in CONCACAF, was one of the key people in the case, leading investigators to his colleagues—including Jack Warner from Trinidad and Tobago—and the private world of illegal payments they were involved in.

From a hotel in Switzerland, up to seven members were quietly taken into custody. Yet, the news around the world was anything but quiet. Even the United States—a country notorious for disregarding international soccer news—ran the story on major outlets (including *ESPN* and *NPR,* to name a few), with follow-up features.

Sepp Blatter, the longtime FIFA president, was defiantly against the accusations, insisting they were false. Allegations of corruption had been leading up to this juncture for years. Michael Zenn-Rufinen, a former high-ranking FIFA member who worked closely with Blatter, came out in the mid-2000s, accusing Blatter of multiple counts of corruption. He was eventually let go.

As fall of 2015 approached, it became clear that Blatter and Michel Platini, who was the president of UEFA at the time, were in cahoots, transferring illegal payments. On October 8, 2015, both Blatter and Platini were suspended by FIFA for 90 days. It was a turn of events that took over news broadcasts around the world, yet again. After trying to recover from the troubles with FIFA five months earlier, things just got worse instead of better for the image of the grand old soccer body. A number of FIFA members requested an emergency Executive Committee meeting to cover their tracks for the time being and to keep the organization of world soccer in place. At that point, Platini was anticipating a move to replace Blatter as FIFA president. This never came to fruition.

The FIFA website described, in brief, the background of interim president, Issa Hayatou (of Cameroon). What many people later realized was that he had allegations of corruption following him since 2010. Essentially, people around the world were saying, "surprise, surprise." Hayatou, born in 1946, was a former soccer and basketball player who became a physical education teacher, later stepping into the role of general secretary of the Cameroonian Football Federation from 1985-88, before becoming the president of the CAF (Confederation African de Football), while also acting as a FIFA vice president since 1992. His immediate task as interim president was pretty clear: desperately try to settle things down while remaining as calm as possible until a vote could take place for the position of full-time FIFA president.

A suspension was also placed on FIFA secretary general, Jerome Valcke. Valcke, Platini, and Blatter had the ban placed on them by the Adjudicatory Chamber of the Ethics Committee, led by Hans Joachim Eckert. For 90 days the ban would block the three men from all national and international soccer-related activities. At the time, FIFA rules stated that after the 90 days went by, there would be an option to continue the ban, but not exceeding 45 days.

To many, the suspension of Blatter, along with the revelations of other corrupt members, was a long time in the making. Drama and international intrigue was really thrown onto Blatter back in May of 2015, as intense investigations promised to bring him to justice. He was trying to avoid all the controversy, hoping to remain president. Things only got worse on October 8, 2015, when he was accused of giving Platini an illegal *payment-bribe-helping hand* of over a million dollars. The payment was not recognized in FIFA's books. UEFA made no urgent attempt to name a replacement president for Platini, noting they would comply with the arrangements made within the FIFA ban of Platini. (After all, the replacement that would have stepped into Platini's shoes, as UEFA interim president, was Angel Villar Llona, who was dealing with an Ethics Committee investigation for not cooperating with an inquiry into the 2018 and 2022 FIFA World Cup bids.)

With humility and disgrace, UEFA announced that Platini would step aside from his official duties, for the time being, as the president of UEFA. As of October 8, 2015, he did not attend UEFA meetings and cancelled multiple business-related trips.

The controversy surrounding Blatter and Platini overshadowed the previous arrests of multiple high-ranking FIFA members, including Blazer and Warner, and those cases were investigated by the FBI and United States Department of Justice headed by US attorney general, Loretta Lynch. In short, the whole thing was spinning out of control.

The world was hit with this news, trying to make sense of what was going on with FIFA. Most people raised an eyebrow when it was announced the 2022 World Cup would be held in the lesser-known country of Qatar. Bribes, kick-backs, racketeering, and ostensibly *double-parking violations for more than ten minutes** were all part of the equation. It's worth repeating that even *ESPN*[24] radio and TV were discussing the events in great detail.

---

* Only a theory. Parking violations seem to go hand-in-hand with larger crimes.

FIFA, of course, has been the longstanding organizing body of world soccer, dating back to 1904. The relatively short list of FIFA presidents has included (beginning with present day): Gianni Infantino, Issa Hayatou, Sepp Blatter, Joao Havalange, Stanley Rous, Ernst Thommen, Arthur Drewry, Rodolphe Seeldrayers, Jules Rimet, Cornelis August Wilhelm Hirschman, Daniel Burley Woolfall, and Robert Guerin. Many of those listed lived in a time when social media and instant news were not as prevalent as they were in Blatter's era.

In the last days of Blatter's reign, there was even a feeling of trepidation for FIFA's possible collapse. Hence, as FIFA organizes the World Cup, there was hint of Russia 2018 possibly being in jeopardy. Since the uproar of the FIFA crimes, things have settled down as the new president, Gianni Infantino—who took office on February 26, 2016—guided the World Cup into Russia. The flurry of press that was hounding Sepp Blatter substantially faded away. And, luckily, the World Cup continues.

A LOOK AHEAD TO WORLD CUP 2026

"32 Teams will Increase to 48"

Originally, in World Cup 1930, there were 13 teams. In 1934, it increased to 16. World Cup 1938 had 15 teams. At Brazil 1950, it went back to 13. From 1954-1978, 16 teams competed. Then, from 1982-1994, 24 teams competed. In 1998, FIFA made it so 32 teams would compete in the tournament. Currently, the number of teams is still 32.

The format for the 2026 World Cup is to have 48 teams compete. FIFA plans to have the system changed from four teams in a group, which is the current format, to three, with the top two advancing into the elimination round. The tournament would still take place in 32 days, and a winning team would still play seven games. FIFA President Infantino might be replaced, and things may change. Or, by then, who knows, perhaps it'll be the start of something great.

2026 WORLD CUP BIDS

Various news outlets reported on April 10, 2017, that the US, Mexico, and Canada were making a joint bid for the 2026 World Cup.

An interview with the US Soccer president, Sunil Gulati, was broadcasted on the *NPR* affiliate *WBEZ Chicago* (91.5FM), and he explained how the US was the most successful host nation in World Cup history in terms of average attendance and total attendance; this was for a number of reasons, including transportation, hotel accommodations, and top-notch stadiums. Gulati did not think President Trump's travel ban (be it temporary or permanent) will have an effect on the decision-making process or the eventual travel plans for people wanting to visit the US for games. He also pointed out that the proposal put forward (for FIFA's consideration) delineated a shared game outline with Mexico and Canada receiving a lesser amount of glamour games,*

---

* This refers to teams that carry more weight based on their current ranking, past record, popularity at large, and star players. A few obvious examples include Brazil, Argentina, and Germany. It also refers to elimination games.

while the US would host the majority, including all games from the semifinals to the final. Just another process within FIFA's agenda as the World Cup continues forward.

WORLD CUP QUALIFICATIONS EXPLAINED

HOW THE 32 TEAMS MADE IT TO RUSSIA 2018

For those who have previously been confused over the World Cup qualification rounds—also referred to in some circles as the "Preliminary Competition"—fear no more! At first glance, they may come across as complicated schemes meant for engineers at NASA, but in reality, they're relatively straightforward. Here is a simple breakdown of the World Cup qualification rounds…

The FIFA World Cup qualifications are broken up into geographical territories: Europe, Africa, North America, Asia, South America, and Oceania. Europe and Africa are the most straightforward.

In Europe, all 54 teams enter qualifications for the World Cup a few years beforehand (September 2016), and they're put into groups (nine in total; Groups A, B, C, D, E, F, G, H, and I) in which they play many games in what FIFA calls "Round One." Each group has six teams. From those groups, the first-place winners, of course, qualify. So that's nine teams. (We don't need Ramanujan, yet.) After that, the top eight second-place finishers have a playoff, referred to as "Round Two," and, from there, four teams join the first-place winners in the World Cup. In the end, 13 teams qualify.

In Africa, teams compete in three rounds for a place in the World Cup. Their gradual elimination process began in October of 2015. Initial games in "Round One" are based on a ranking system with lower-ranked teams playing one another first. The winners of "Round One" meet more teams in "Round Two" where more teams are eliminated. Finally, "Round Three" consists of five groups—A, B, C, D, and E—that represent the last stage of qualifications. Eventually, the top team of each group represents Africa. End the end, five teams qualify.

North America and Asia have a similar setup to one another. In North America, the lower-ranked teams battle it out until they meet the higher-ranked teams (who were comfortably waiting with byes). As they meet, many rounds are played, five in total (which began in March 2015), and teams are eventually eliminated until six are left. That's the final round, called the "Hexagonal," or "Hex," for short. Of those six, the top three qualify for the World Cup, and the fourth-place team has a playoff game—the intercontinental playoff—with a team from Asia, and that team, whoever wins, goes to the World Cup as well. In the end, 3 ½ teams qualify. (Or, three with a possible fourth.)

In Asia, the qualification games began in March 2015. The lower-ranked teams fight it out. Then they meet the higher-ranked teams for a place in the World Cup. Three rounds are played. By "Round Three" there are two groups left—A and B—each with six teams. They compete, and the top two teams from each group advance to the World Cup. The two third-place teams from each group still have a chance and play one another in a "Round Four" playoff. The winner of this playoff represents Asia in another playoff—the intercontinental playoff—with a team from CONCACAF (North America) for a final chance at the World Cup. In the end, 4 ½ teams qualify. (Or, four with a possible fifth.)

In South America, all 10 teams play each other in ongoing games in one long round (which began in October 2015), and the top four teams qualify for the World Cup. The fifth ranked team has a playoff with an Oceania team to decide who advances to the World Cup. In the end, 4 ½ teams qualify. (Or, four with a possible fifth.)

Oceania gets what FIFA calls half a berth. The lower-ranked teams battle it out, and one team moves on to compete with the higher-ranked teams. During three rounds, many games are played (which began in August 2015). In the end, for "Round 3," six teams remain, and they are placed into two groups (A and B). The eventual winner moves on to the intercontinental playoff; this representative must get past the fifth ranked team from South America to have a chance at attending the World Cup. (Or, as FIFA says, half a berth.)

The rankings for each Confederation in cooperation with FIFA were determined from around 2014 and 2015. Essentially, in the complicated world of FIFA and their relationship with each Confederation, as far as rankings go for World Cup qualifications, "It would be up to each Confederation," said Logan, an employee with the United States Soccer Federation, based in Chicago, on June 6, 2017, over the phone. And the rankings, of course, are based on team performance. So it's always important for teams to win. That's why teams are always calling "unimportant" games "important." Rankings matter in the long run.

For verification of the qualification process, the headquarters of CONCACAF—based in Miami Beach, Florida—were contacted on June 6, 2017. Rebecca—who answered the phone—would not release anyone's name for comment on World Cup qualifications. Nor would she provide an official person's email. She only provided a general email.* When politely pressed for any official's name at CONCACAF for future reference, she pushed the call to another woman named Marjorie. Marjorie explained she was only part of an answering service. When asked, "Who is the president of CONCACAF?" Margerie got agitated and said, "You'll have to look that up online. I don't have no information on the company." All in all, for a few easy questions, they were very unhelpful, guarded, suspicious, and rude.

For the record, an online account gave this version of CONCACAF's president:

"In May 2012, Cayman Islands banker Jeffrey Webb was installed as President of CONCACAF. On 27 May. 2015, Webb was arrested in Zurich, Switzerland on corruption charges in the U.S.

Victor Montagliani, leader of the Canadian Soccer Association, was elected as President of CONCACAF in May 2016."[25]

For anyone that may be concerned with the technicalities of the qualification process—and the relationship between FIFA and Confederations along the way—just know that there are checks

---

* An email was sent that day, seeking confirmation of the CONCACAF relationship with FIFA regarding the World Cup qualification process. A week was requested for a response, and nothing came back in that time.

and balances which keep it all in place. The Confederations are in contact with FIFA on a regular basis, and Confederations may come up with their qualification schemes on their own, but, clearly, hypothetically, if they're way out of whack, FIFA would be able to enter the equation and suggest a way to make it realistic. As things stand, the process seems to be in accord with the soccer-playing world. What may be confusing, from time to time, are the myriad of games, and ongoing rounds.

Could TV* do a better job drawing out the process? Definitely, yes. Many times, if not all the time, TV announcers will glaze over the intricacies of the qualification rounds verbally with no map. (They like to get straight into highlights, which is understandable.) Would it help viewers understand the simplicity of the process if soccer TV announcers had a large map of the ongoing qualifications, and returned to it often? Probably. After all, it's the World Cup qualification process, which, in essence, is the World Cup.

As the years move on, dates for the World Cup qualification process may change. The number of teams allowed in the World Cup may change as well. Naturally, this would affect the World Cup qualification process. Regardless, the same concept remains. It's all dwindled down through a series of rankings, rounds, eliminations, and further rounds, with further games. It's like having the World Cup over a two-year span.

With as many teams as there are, FIFA takes a difficult process and makes it quite manageable. FIFA's website keeps all games up to date. Thanks FIFA!

---

* In large part, this is referring to American television outlets.

With that said, the race for World Cup Russia began years in advance with many rounds and many games. October and November 2017 were the last qualification rounds.* In October, things finished up. And, in November, the last remaining teams competed in playoff games, which is always exciting. By then, it was clear which 32 teams made the 2018 World Cup.

It was in November of 2017 that FIFA announced the four pots:

- Pot 1: Russia, Germany, Brazil, Portugal, Argentina, Belgium, Poland, and France
- Pot 2: Spain, Peru, Switzerland, England, Colombia, Mexico, Uruguay, and Croatia
- Pot 3: Denmark, Iceland, Costa Rica, Sweden, Tunisia, Egypt, Senegal, and Iran
- Pot 4: Serbia, Nigeria, Australia, Japan, Morocco, Panama, South Korea (Korea Republic), and Saudi Arabia

Following that, on December 1, 2017, at the State Kremlin Palace in Moscow, the actual draw was made. Always a big ordeal, FIFA announced the event on its website: "Gary Lineker and Maria Komandnaya to conduct Final Draw."†

---

* In the case of the 2022 World Cup, two final months, likely October and November of 2021, will be paramount; in World Cup 2026, two final months, likely October and November of 2025, will be paramount, and so on. FIFA may change October and November to, say, September and October, or November and December. Essentially, the larger point is this: Two final months wrap up the qualification process all around the world.

† Accessed from http://www.fifa.com/worldcup/index.html on November 19, 2017.

In summary, that's the qualification process. Long and arduous? Yes, but tractable. So, as it turns out, Andrew Wiles, Ken Ribet, Gauss, Newton, and Eratosthenes weren't needed, after all.

10 INTERESTING FACTS ABOUT THE 2018 FIFA WORLD CUP

1. This is the second World Cup to use goal-line technology. The first was Brazil 2014.

2. To this point in history, only teams from Europe and South America have won the World Cup.

3. As of 2018, the United States is the only North American team to ever take third place in a World Cup. They achieved this in 1930.

4. As of 2018, the only Asian team to ever place in the top four is South Korea. They placed fourth in 2002.

5. The official ball will be provided by adidas.

6. This is the first time Russia will host the World Cup.

7. This is the first time a country that stretches from Europe and Asia will host.

8. Despite not winning a World Cup in soccer, Russia—including its past with the former Soviet Union—has contributed a great deal to the world of hockey, basketball,

traditional Olympic sports, and, the "less athletic world," but a competitive one nonetheless, of chess, particularly from 1948 on, in the World Chess Championship.

9. The Russian stadiums are located in the western half of the huge country.

10. Moscow, the capitol of Russia, will provide two stadiums.

CHAPTER 4

BACKGROUND ON RUSSIA

A LOOK AT RUSSIA—GENERAL OVERVIEW

Russia's landscape—which encompasses the largest country on earth—stretches from Western Europe all the way to Eastern Asia, just a short jaunt to Alaska. Within this geographic expanse, featuring grassy plains, mountains, lakes, great rivers, access to oceans, arctic wildlife, oil, minerals, and vast forests, is a complex history, which today, with a population of around 144 million, is reflected by a multitude of unique cultures, including the Kalmyks, Komi, Armenians, Yakuts, and Cossacks, to name a few. From their vast array of citizens, Russia has contributed a great deal in the areas of science, space travel, math, music, chess, art, and athletics. Much of Russia's history will be on display during World Cup 2018, expressed by the few lucky cities hosting the games.

A BRIEF LOOK AT EACH VENUE—RUSSIAN STADIUMS AND LOCAL HISTORY

(All stadium capacities are approximate.[26])

MOSCOW, RUSSIA

- **Luzhniki Stadium**
- **Capacity: 78,360**

Luzhniki Stadium was chosen as the focal point of the tournament, serving as the setting for the opening game to be held on June 14 and the championship to be held on July 15, 2018 (with other matches in between). It's beautifully located in Moscow next to the Moskva River.

LOCAL PRO TEAM

In recent years, Luzhniki Stadium has largely hosted Russian national team games. Whereas, it was previously used by a few pro teams, including PFC CSKA Moscow* (founded in 1911), who switched to Arena CSKA, or VEB Arena,[27] as it's also known, and Spartak Moscow (founded in 1922), who now play in the Otkrytiye Arena.

HISTORICAL OVERVIEW

Originally, Luzhniki Stadium was built in 1955, opening in 1956 as the Central Lenin Stadium (known as such from 1956-1992), named in honor of Vladimir Lenin, the first leader of the Soviet Union (who held office from 1922-24). It was rebuilt between 2013-2017 and holds a capacity of just over 78,000. Representing Russian soccer, CSKA Moscow won the coveted UEFA Cup in the 2005-2004 season.

IN BETWEEN GAMES

Saint Basil's Cathedral of Moscow is a beautiful tourist destination that compliments the stadiums with a taste of Russian culture.

---

* Which stands for: Professional Football Club, Central Sport Club of the Army, Moscow.

MOSCOW, RUSSIA

- **Otkrytiye Arena (Spartak Stadium)**
- **Capacity: 45,360**

For the 2017 Confederations Cup and 2018 World Cup, Otkrytiye Arena will be known simply as the Spartak Stadium. The structure was built in 2010 and opened in 2014.

LOCAL PRO TEAM

Spartak Moscow plays its games here.

HISTORICAL OVERVIEW

The ground that soccer fans will be walking on has a fascinating backstory. Prior to the more recent history in connection with the Soviet Union, settlements in and around Moscow began long before the city's founding in 1147 AD. Archaeological remains of rudimentary beginnings go all the way back to the Neolithic period.

By the 9th century AD, the Volga trade route—which was galvanized by Vikings—operated in conjunction with the Volga and Oka Rivers, enabling Northwest Russia to establish trade connections with Northern Europe and people of the south, including but not limited to areas around the Caspian Sea; this activity incorporated the region around what would become Moscow.

In 1147 AD, Yuri Dolgorukiy (son of Vladimir II Monomakh[28]) and Sviatoslav Olgovich (son of Oleg Svyatoslavich[29]), who was prince of Novgorod, met in Moscow, establishing one of the first records of the future city. Yuri, in 1156 AD, established a fort on the site, which was later demolished by the Mongols. About a hundred years later, during the 1260s, Daniel of Moscow (the son of Alexander Nevsky[30]), reestablished the fort, laying further groundwork for what would be Moscow, the eventual capital of Russia.

Now, years later, soccer is a big part of the culture in Moscow. Spartak Moscow has won the Soviet Cup—which later turned into the Russian Cup—thirteen times, last claiming victory in 2003.

IN BETWEEN GAMES

Timeout Rooftop Bar, Bosco Bar, Dream Bar, and others will be available in Moscow for soccer fans as the World Cup celebration marches on.

SAINT PETERSBURG, RUSSIA

- **Krestovsky Stadium (Saint Petersburg Stadium)**
- **Capacity: 68,134**

Construction for the stadium began in 2007 and was completed in 2017. It rests on Krestovsky Island. It has a very intimate seating arrangement—elegant blue-colored seats of essentially two tiers—and spectators are right on top of the action.

LOCAL PRO TEAM

FC Zenit Saint Petersburg founded in 1925. Others might say 1914.

HISTORICAL OVERVIEW

Saint Petersburg,* which sits on the Baltic Sea, has been a strategic location for Russia for years. It was founded in 1703 by Peter the Great after defeating Sweden in the Great Northern War. Under Peter the Great (who was also known as Peter Alexeyevich and Tsar Peter), who lived from 1672-1725, Russia modernized much of its culture with influences from the Enlightenment. Peter saw the need for a great naval presence in the world. Much of his vision for Russia was inspired by everything that was going on in Western Europe, partly from a tour in which he famously went incognito, eventually studying shipbuilding in the Netherlands. Among other things, he also established the Russian Academy of Sciences in Saint Petersburg in 1724.

In today's world, FC Zenit Saint Petersburg is the most popular sporting team in town. In the 2007-2008 season, they took home the UEFA Cup in what was an amazing, historic run for their team.

IN BETWEEN GAMES

Soccer travelers might want to see the Hermitage Museum and Winter Palace in Saint Petersburg. Also of interest is the Yusupov Palace, a well-known tourist destination that many soccer fans may gravitate toward between games.

---

* Its name was changed to Petrograd in 1914 at the beginning of WWI, then to Leningrad in 1924, following the death of Vladimir Lenin, and back to Saint Petersburg in 1991, following the collapse of the Soviet Union.

World Cup tourists might stumble across a few bars, including Saigon, Beer Diet, Al Capone Bar, and Room 13.

KALININGRAD, RUSSIA

- **Kaliningrad Stadium**
- **Capacity: 35,000**

Construction for the stadium went from 2015-2017. It has a projected capacity of 35,000.

LOCAL PRO TEAM

FC Baltika Kaliningrad founded in 1954.

HISTORICAL OVERVIEW

The area is known for Old Prussians, which refers to tribes of people from the Baltic Sea region (separate from the German state of Prussia, circa 1525-1947 AD). There is some mention of their territories in Ptolemy's attempt to map Europe during the 2nd century AD.

During the Middle Ages, a settlement was established, referred to as Twangste. Though, by 1255 AD, the Teutonic Knights took over during the Northern Crusades, establishing a new fortress called Konigsberg.

In WWII, British bombing raids damaged much of the city. Following the war, and the subsequent Potsdam Conference agreements made by the Allies,* the city fell into the hands of the USSR. In 1946, the name was changed to Kaliningrad.

Today, the local pro soccer team is extremely important for local pride. FC Baltika Kaliningrad's team colors are white and blue.

IN BETWEEN GAMES

The Konigsberg Cathedral is a well-known tourist stop in Kaliningrad.

Bykov Bar is one of many choices soccer fans will have while visiting Kaliningrad.

KAZAN, RUSSIA

- **Kazan Arena**
- **Capacity: 45,379**

Kazan Arena began construction in 2010. It was completed in 2013, costing approximately $450 million. Architects got creative, as an entrance sits a few hundred feet below the curved top of the arena, as if entering an underground tavern.

The arena played host to the 2013 Summer Universiade, an array of different athletic competitions (similar to the Olympics) for university students representing 162 countries from around the world. Russia led all nations with 156 gold medals. In 2015, the World Aquatics Championships were held in the arena, and

---

* The USSR, the United States, and England.

prior to World Cup 2018, it also welcomed games from the 2017 Confederations Cup.

LOCAL PRO TEAM

FC Rubin Kazan founded in 1958.

HISTORICAL OVERVIEW

Kazan is known as the "Third Capital" of Russia, a request granted to them by the Russian Patent Office in 2009. The seven districts of Kazan are: Aviastroitelny, Vakhitovsky, Kirovsky, Moskovsky, Novo-Savinovsky, Privolzhsky, and Sovetsky. Anyone traveling from Kazan International Airport to the city would possibly take bus route 97, which connects the two.

FC Rubin Kazan won the Russian Cup in the 2011-2012 season.

IN BETWEEN GAMES

World Cup fans might travel around the city on rapid transit by using the Kazan Metro. Barvikha Lounge Bar and The Woods Craft Bar are among the many choices of bars in Kazan.

NIZHNY NOVGOROD, RUSSIA

- **Nizhny Novgorod Stadium**
- **Capacity: 44,899**

Anticipating the World Cup, the stadium was built in haste between 2015-2017.

LOCAL PRO TEAM

FC Volga Nizhny Novgorod (1998-2016).

HISTORICAL OVERVIEW

Nizhny Novgorod was founded in 1221 AD (take that Delaware!), as Yuri II established a settlement near the confluence of the Oka and Volga rivers. Located a little bit east of Moscow, deep in the heartland of Russia, commerce was flourishing here in the illustrious 1800s, making it one of the largest trade centers in the Russian Empire.

FC Volga Nizhny Novgorod was also known as the Volga Natives.

IN BETWEEN GAMES

World Cup tourists may notice the *Nizhegorodskaya Pravda,* a longstanding newspaper in town. There are many bars for World Cup fans to visit, including Kraken Bar.

SAMARA, RUSSIA

- **Cosmos Arena (Samara Arena)**
- **Capacity: 44,918**

Construction for the arena went from 2014-2018, just making it for the World Cup, for a cost of around $320 million. It was built in lieu of Metallurg Stadium, which had been in use since 1957 and was home to the club team FC Krylia Sovetov Samara.

Building an arena is a complicated business. Many parties are involved, including the government, contractors, organizing bodies, banks, lenders, environmentalists, lawyers, and citizens who all bring their ideas, criticisms, and suggestions. All arena bids must go through FIFA, who helps weigh out the decision-making process.

The original plans for the new stadium to be built on an island just south of the city were eighty-sixed as it wasn't in a good location and lacked a bridge setup. Instead, the site for the arena was chosen closer to the city center. This hurdle made the project extra-challenging, especially with a deadline that happens to coincide with billions of anxious people tuning in from every corner of the globe to watch the most popular sport in the world. They say learning a new language is one of the hardest things to do in life. Try building a new stadium in time for the World Cup. But, like the Moscow Metro of 1935,* they got it done with hard work and good old-fashioned Russian persistence, just in time for all the festivities and competitions.

LOCAL PRO TEAM

Founded in 1942, FC Krylia Sovetov Samara plays its games here.

HISTORIC OVERVIEW

Samara is a bit north of the Caspian Sea near the border of Kazakhstan. The city's name has roots in the Neolithic Samara

---

* Unlike the circumstances surrounding the 1935 Metro, for the construction of Samara Arena, no British engineers were arrested for suspicion of espionage.

culture, dating to around 4,000-5,000 BC. It is thought that the region represents the birthplace of the Proto-Indo-European language.

Established in 1586 AD, Samara and the immediate area served as a protective base against roaming attackers on Russia's eastern frontier. It was a place of geographic importance, considering the Volga and Samara Rivers. They served as convenient routes of transportation while also providing a theater for pirate attacks.

In the modern era of soccer, a much tamer time (though, some might argue to the contrary), FC Krylia Sovetov Samara hired coach Vadim Skripchenko in 2016.

IN BETWEEN GAMES

Of the many interesting things to do in Samara in between games, World Cup fans might find themselves visiting Stalin's Bunker, an underground shelter and meeting place. Patrik Pub might be a bar soccer fans visit. Or, possibly, they'll find themselves in the Pizza Kit for a drink and bite to eat.

VOLGOGRAD, RUSSIA

- **Volgograd Arena**
- **Capacity: 45,568**

Volgograd Arena's construction took place from 2015-2017 over the grounds of the previous Central Stadium (which was around since 1958) and at the base of the Mamayev Kurgan memorial site, which is located on ground high above the city and honors the Battle of Stalingrad from WWII.

LOCAL PRO TEAM

FC Rotor Volgograd plays its games here. They were established in 1929.

HISTORIC OVERVIEW

Founded in 1589 AD, "Tsaritsyn" represented a trading post and fortress on Russia's southern border, which was full of tumultuous activity. In 1925, it changed names to Stalingrad in honor of Joseph Stalin.

The history of this city can stop you in your tracks with awe and wonderment. In 1942, in the midst of WWII as Nazi forces invaded the USSR, the Battle of Stalingrad* epitomized the struggle on the Eastern Front. It produced heavy casualties with estimates of up to 2,000,000 dead, possibly more, making it one of the most costly battles in history.

Then, in 1961, under the direction of Nikita Khrushchev (leader of the Soviet Union from 1953-1964), the city's name of Stalingrad was replaced with Volgograd—which translates to Volga City, representing the Volga River nearby—in an attempt to lessen the strength of Stalin's previous reign of power.

Soccer has been a passion in the city for years. FC Rotor Volgograd had a string of second-place finishes in the King's

---

* August 23, 1942, to February 2, 1943.

Cup,* three years in a row: 1989, 1990, and 1991. Finally, they won it in 1995.

IN BETWEEN GAMES

During the 2018 World Cup, some fans might be staying at the Hampton by Hilton. Of the many bars to choose from, Doubler Pub might be a stopping place for traveling soccer fans.

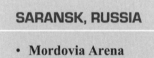

SARANSK, RUSSIA

- **Mordovia Arena**
- **Capacity: 45,015**

Construction of the fully equipped arena took place from 2010 to 2017 for about $300 million.

LOCAL PRO TEAM

Established in 1961, FC Mordovia Saransk plays in this arena.

HISTORIC OVERVIEW

The city has roots dating back to 1641 AD. This was a few years after the establishment of the House of Romanov, which, as a dynasty, presided over Russia from 1613-1917 AD. (The first Russian dynasty was the House of Rurik, which lasted from approximately 862-1610 AD.)

---

* A tournament held in Thailand.

Soccer fans saw Andrei Syomin become coach of FC Mordovia Saransk in 2017.

IN BETWEEN GAMES

There should be many festivities and places to eat in Saransk while fans enjoy the World Cup. On route to World Cup games, some visitors might go past the Church of St. Nicholas.

ROSTOV-ON-DON, RUSSIA

- **Rostov Arena**
- **Capacity: 45,000**

The Rostov Arena was put together from 2014 to 2017.

LOCAL PRO TEAM

FC Rostov was established back in 1930.

HISTORIC OVERVIEW

Rostov-on-Don sits on the Don River, next to the Sea of Azov, which borders the Black Sea. It's an area that has been part of trade and military conquest dating back to the ancient Greeks who called the nomadic people there "Scythians." The historian, Herodotus, who may not have actually visited the territories of Scythia, noted their name was "Scoloti."[31] This land would have encompassed parts of what is modern-day Ukraine and southwestern Russia. By 1749 AD, a strategic outpost was made by Empress Elizabeth.

Because of its geographic relevance with railroads and natural resources, such as oil, the Germans contested the area during WWII. More recently, partly because of the turmoil between Russia and the region of Donbass, Ukraine, Rostov-on-Don has been called Europe's most dangerous city, according to Wikipedia,[32] the Mirror (of the UK),[33] and the Coventry Telegraph.[34] From early 2017, a good year before the World Cup (a lot can change in a year!), the top ten list of dangerous and crime-infested cities in Europe read like this: (1) Rostov-on-Don; (2) Bari, Italy; (3) Turin, Italy; (4) Naples, Italy (get your act together, Italy); (5) Marseilles, France; (6) Lille, France; (7) Coventry, England; (8) Rotterdam, Netherlands; (9) Glasgow, Scotland; and (10) Sarajevo, Bosnia and Herzegovina.

No big deal. After all, what's being number one? It's usually a fleeting moment in time, anyway. It's hard to stay on top. Just ask Mark-Paul Gosselaar. By the looks of it, Italy should have the top spot in no time. Despite this ranking, Russian authorities are eager to show off the historic area, confident it will add plenty of festive beauty to the coveted World Cup.

FC Rostov had a great year in the 2013-2014 season, winning the Russian Cup for the first time.

IN BETWEEN GAMES

Rostov-on-Don has many places to stop for a drink and snack during the World Cup, such as Billi Bons, and the streets should be lively with action.

SOCHI, RUSSIA

- **Fisht Olympic Stadium**
- **Capacity: 47,659**

The stadium opened in 2013 at a cost of around $779 million, and it was set aside for multiple uses, including the 2014 Winter Olympics, the 2014 Paralympics, and the 2017 Confederations Cup.

LOCAL PRO TEAM

FC Sochi was founded in 2013. (Apparently, they play in a different stadium: the Sochi Central Stadium, which has a capacity of just over 10,000.)

HISTORIC OVERVIEW

Joseph Stalin kept a "Yacha" or second home in Sochi.

FC Sochi hired Khazret Dyshekov as their coach in 2016. It is unknown whether he has a second home in Sochi, or not.

IN BETWEEN GAMES

In beautiful Sochi, there are many things to do and see. Bar London is one of many bars that World Cup fans can visit in between games.

YEKATERINBURG, RUSSIA

- **Central Stadium (Yekaterinburg Arena)**
- **Capacity: 35,000**

Originally built in 1957, renovations on the stadium were made from 2006-2011 and then again from 2014-2017.

LOCAL PRO TEAM

FC Ural Yekaterinburg established in 1930.

HISTORIC OVERVIEW

Yekaterinburg was founded in 1723 AD by Vasily Tatishchev (a distant relative of Prince Rurik and author of Russia's history) and Georg Wilhelm de Gennin (a Russian military leader). The former CSKA Moscow standout and Soviet national team member, Aleksandr Tarkhanov, began coaching FC Ural Yekaterinburg in 2016.

IN BETWEEN GAMES

Possibly World Cup fans will stop by a place called Palekh for a drink and a bite to eat.

These beautiful cities and stadiums—starting with Saint Petersburg in the north, Kaliningrad in the west, Yekaterinburg in the east, down to Sochi in the south, and those in between—make up the landscape of games for World Cup Russia. While tourists from around the world will be walking on their grounds, each game will contribute to the final whistle. From Moscow—one of the key cities in Russian and world history—a new World Cup champion will emerge.

CLOSING WORDS

The great country of Russia represents a unique place in history for hosting the FIFA World Cup, which, in turn, represents "the best game in the world," "the people's game," "the beautiful game," or, soccer. A beautiful capsule in time, World Cup Russia will now step in line with all the World Cups that preceded it... every grand tournament, from Sweden 1958, Spain 1982, the United States 1994, Germany 2006, and Brazil 2014, to now.

From the rubber tires of planes touching down at airports, to the sound of the first whistle, to the first ball struck by a shiny $300 dollar shoe, to the fastidious detail of each uniform design, to each individual beer produced by breweries around the world for millions of eager fans, with every kind of soda, water, wine, and food variety from a myriad of companies, along with virtually every possible commodity that can be intertwined with the largest tournament known to man…the games will be watched by billions of people on TVs, computers, and mobile devices from all around the globe. Everyone involved is subject to every last detail, to enjoy a game, and be part of something epic with roots dating back to the first tournament in 1930.

Today we have Messi, Neymar, and Cristiano Ronaldo, following in the footsteps of Pele, Garrincha, Maradona, Matthäus,

Romario, and many others. And, yes, new stars will emerge. The platform for the arrival of fresh talent is provided for in every World Cup, Russia included. And then Russia will subside, just like Chile, Mexico, France, and South Africa, becoming an enchanted memory.

As World Cup Qatar comes around in 2022, along with those that follow, a chapter in history will be established not only for the beautiful game, but also for all the world, representing the greatest virtues on earth. The World Cup is one of a kind. The impact it's had on humanity is tantamount to any assortment of past human accomplishments, activities, or symbolic epochs, in league with the Great Pyramids, Stonehenge, the first Olympic Games in Greece, the Aztec, Maya, and Inca civilizations and all the marvels they produced, the Great Wall of China, Ankor Wat in Cambodia, Easter Island, ancient Rome, the Renaissance, the Industrial Revolution, the Digital Revolution, and, if possible, everything in between. As a by-product of globalization, the World Cup rivals the beauty of those places and eras in a profound way while also incorporating the very essence of their discoveries and inventions in the form of stadiums (and architecture), technology (and the live coverage of games in real-time thanks to electromagnetism, computers, microchips, integrated circuits, television, wireless advancements, satellites, and smart phones), art, irrigation, transportation (including cars, planes, trains, helicopters, drones with cameras), while showcasing the human drive to perform through athletics and achieve immortality.

As a future relic, every aspect of the World Cup—right down to the tiny pieces of concrete from the stadiums—has the allure of a three-pound block of gold found deep in a cave somewhere in a South American jungle stumbled upon by Colonel Fawcett. It's one of those events filled with spectacular moments that will attract future historians and laymen that share a passion for stadiums, stars, stories, high stakes, competition, winners, losers, and the ultimate prize. They'll look back in time and see the most popular sport and the highest tournament at their very best.

To look back at the past is grand, yet, to have it right now, in the moment, is something else *special*. The World Cup isn't just a tournament. Like Sumerian cuneiform and the Mayan Ballgame and Carl Sagan sending Voyager into the unknown universe with the Golden Record…it's history being made. To many people, it's a religion; it's larger than life itself.

Russia 2018 has taken its place among the few elite countries on earth to host the beautiful game and to be a part of the ongoing story for all time.

APPENDIX

BONUS MATERIAL

GERMANY

ATTENTION TO DETAIL AND POSSESSION PASSING

Many people have sat around wondering how Germany could remain so steady for so long. They must have a style, an approach that sets them apart. Like Argentina, Brazil, and Italy, their determination and organization seems to set them apart from most competitors.

Generally speaking, the Germans and Italians share a passion for getting small details on the field just right. Other teams share this pursuit, but for years the Germans and Italians have led world soccer. Could it have something to do with their culture? A culture with a tradition of engineers…

People all around the world make pottery, which is a skilled pursuit. But it's not like making a car. Constructing a car is a whole different world of complexity. One that requires many different people with different skillsets all bringing their ideas together to form a beautiful piece of "moving art." Many countries make cars. But not every country makes high-end cars with immaculate detail. Like a fine-tuned BMW or Porsche, which requires a multitude of engineering techniques to achieve perfection, the Germans have applied the same systematic approach to their soccer program.

When it comes to engineering, things have to be just right. There's a right way, and a wrong way. (Take it from the co-founder of Apple, Steve Wozniak, who liked repeating digits. On early circuit boards that he created, he would scratch certain prototypes in order to make it more beautiful, placing the chips in the perfect position, with five holes for the chips in a board, versus eight holes, which was his original design, as he spent two weeks taking the board apart, to make way for only five holes, saying, "It had to be that artistically perfect to me.") Engineering, in general, demands fastidious attention to detail. After all, Mercedes, BMW, and Porsche aren't known for low-grade designs. Such a pursuit to achieve perfection and get all the parts of the car just the right way would naturally spill over to the cultural fabric of society.

When it comes to their soccer approach, it seems as though the Germans apply similar engineering techniques, paying close attention to detail, such as the proper technique of players, along with what works and what doesn't work in terms of the flow of play and the chemistry between players. Many people with different skillsets—coaches, trainers, dieticians, strength and conditioning experts, along with shoe designers—come together in a pursuit to create the best players possible, like "moving art."

Where other countries have failed, the Germans have paid close attention to such detail when it comes to developing their players across a broad spectrum (from youth to pro ranks). As such, they've created a congruent system so that any number of players could ostensibly represent the national team, equipped with the proper training to achieve a style of play that has been proven to work over the ages. And, as time has gone on, German coaches and analysts have been perspicacious to work with developing trends in the game in order to stay ahead of the curve.

People such as Paul Breitner—the former West German World Cup champion of 1974—have seized opportunities to take advice from the play of Spain in the 2000s in order to keep Germany relevant with the fluctuating styles of the modern game. Breitner and others found the game was changing in its quickness of pace, and, more specifically, in the decision-making of players.

When watching a well-tuned German team, sometimes the game seems to slow down; the ball is moving slowly between players as they connect pass after pass, but this is part of the quickness of play they've adopted, which is actually improving the decision-making of players and the passing combinations between them which will in affect slow the pace of the game down. In short: The quicker players think, the slower they can make the game.* By implementing this trend, the Germans take the game away from their opponents, which

---

* The paradox of a team like Germany or Spain is that when the players are seen slowly passing the ball around, which Spain is much more accustomed to doing, it's actually a result of thinking very quickly, and, in many cases, playing a pass early with softer touch. In doing so, by increasing the frequency of passes between players, a team can seem to slow the game down, which sounds a bit like Einstein's Twin Paradox.

is part of their longstanding success. Many teams go right for goal, engaging a back-and-forth with their opponent. Unless there's an obvious fast break, that's not the German approach.

Traditionally, German teams have excelled at possession soccer, which involves passing with precision, sound technique, team organization, and combination passing, which requires knowledgeable players and quick thinking. So it's not just individuals thinking quickly, it's everyone as a team thinking quickly, together increasing the frequency of passes within a smaller amount of time in smaller spaces. Where the Germans have succeeded in this regard, many other nations have not caught on. Increasing the pace of play for some teams is usually interpreted to mean running faster and passing the ball harder; everything is charging forward. As opposed to passing the ball across the field with intricate passing combinations, which requires quick thinking. Anyone can move the ball downfield with a quick pace; just forcing it down the line or using a long ball across the field can achieve this, but it's a matter of what a team does after that which is important. This is where most teams get stuck. They've played a successful ball across the field or down the line, and now they're without a plan. Combination passing in small spaces on the field is the key, which is partly why the Germans have separated themselves as one of the great teams to watch. In World Cup Russia, this approach to the game will be on full display, and it's one of the reasons Germany is a favorite to win the whole thing.

GERMAN SOCCER MOVING FORWARD

As far as going forward, Germany doesn't look like they're slowing down. Coming off the 2017 Confederations Cup championship, they keep finding big wins.

To most nations, the record of the Germans from 1996-2002 would be outstanding. In 1996, Germany won the European Cup. In 2002, they got second place in the World Cup. However, in 1998, the Germans left the World Cup early, losing in the quarterfinals, and in the 2000 European Cup they were eliminated in the first round. Imagine the victory dances occurring in Romania should they have had such a run! Not for the Germans, though. It was a down time. They wanted more. Like Brazil, second wasn't good enough. Two bad tournaments following a European championship wasn't going to work.

They keep moving forward, setting the trends, following the trends, learning new ways to stay on top, developing players while always thinking at least twenty years down the road. To them, 1974 is relevant with 2010; there's something to be learned there. By studying different eras and styles, they can apply what worked in the past, combining those methods with the modern game. For instance, they realized that developing an outside attack with the outside defenders was something to improve upon from the era of 1954 with Kohlmeyer and Posipal to Breitner* and Vogts in 1974 to using Lahm and Howedes more liberally in 2014, similar to how the Brazilians have used the position (in the sense that they were so valuable with possession in the half-court offense,† along with productive runs down the line with intelligent passes into the box, as opposed to random crosses, which the English can be guilty of more often than not). From the guidance of coaches Rudy Voeller to Joachim Löw, the teams have adapted to find the right tune of music for any given time.

---

*   Breitner was a versatile outside midfielder as well.

†   The attacking half of the field.

Being part of a great soccer culture is to inherit past success. But this is a tricky topic to understand. It can't be guaranteed that by merely inheriting the great record of previous German teams that the present team—whoever that may be—will live up to the expectations and embody the success of the past players. However, learning from their experiences should allot any German side an upper hand over most opponents. By studying the teams from 1954, 1974, 1990, and 2014—along with plenty of salient efforts in between—this has proven to be true. The German soccer program is a system that stays current with the evolving game, developing players that have an uncanny "in the moment understanding"; that conduct fluid passing connections; that accept the mantra of "everyone's the star" mentality. Their transition from one generation to the next has set the standard. Any changing of the guard should carry over with ease for some time to come, giving Germany an open road to the finals for as long as they see fit. Having said that, World Cup Russia is a chance for Germany to prove, yet again, that their methods work.

SPAIN

THEY WERE ALWAYS GOOD

Someday, Spain has to return to earth! They have to. They've been too good! There have been signs that they're losing the strength they exuded from 2006-2013 (give or take). Yet, Spain is going to cherish their span of good fortune for as long as they can. After all, they've waited a long time to be on top.

For Spain to come back to earth is basically insinuating they were never "that good" to begin with, and that it's kind of a shock that they dominated as they did. This is far from true. Along with turning into possibly the best team ever to roam the earth (2008-2012), since the 1920s, Spain has always been a leader in world competitions, but clearly not on par with the Golden Generation.* No single team or "dynasty" has been that good in international soccer competitions, with three major tournament wins in a row that include a World Cup. (Other than possibly Brazil, with the World Cup title in 2002, followed by Copa America championships in 2004 and 2007.†)

Spain's past results were good, and, as *Soccernomics*[35] asserts, the results were good even considering their resources and population and the isolation period during General Franco's reign from 1936 to 1975, allowing some of the world in but leaving the country much more secluded than they needed to be in soccer terms. From the 1920s to the 2000s, Spain's winning percentage went from a high 78% in the 1920s to higher still 81% in the 2000s, while lingering in competitive limbo during the decades in between. The book *Soccernomics* explains another interesting phenomenon surrounding Spain's reputation as a classic "underachiever" on the world stage: "We calculated that Spain, given its population, income, and experience in the 1980-2001 period, 'should' have scored on average 0.3 goals per game more than its opponents. But Spain did much better than that: it outscored opponents by nearly 0.9 goals, averaging nearly 0.6 goals more than expected.

---

* The Golden Generation refers to the Spanish teams that won Euro 2008, World Cup 2010, and Euro 2012, which carried over many of the same players.

† One salient issue critiques might have with this comparison is the European Cup is arguably far more competitive than the Copa America.

Of the teams that played at least one hundred games in this period, Spain was the eighth-best overperformer in the world. The country was an overachiever long before it began winning prizes. Until very recently, it just wasn't quite big or rich or experienced or lucky enough to win anything."[36]

Most people knew they were always good with the tagline: "Underachievers." In recent generations, their style, of course, has roots in Dutch influences, including Ajax's system where Cruyff was trained, and when he took over Barcelona—which turned out to be just as lucrative for Spain as it was for Barcelona—he brought his bag of tricks along for the ride. For Spain it was a perfect fit. They already had a crafty pass-oriented approach to the game, which relied on skill and grace as opposed to pure brute force. As of 1966, Spain, with Suarez, Gento, and Peiro, had a thoughtful mindset along with a skillful style, but they were playing without the constant frequency of the Tiki-Taka approach.

The Golden Generation benefited from Cruyff's insight, which was in the works before most of the players were even born. It started with Cruyff's arrival as a player with Barcelona in 1973, coached then by the Dutch legend, Rinus Michels. Along with help from others, by the time Cruyff became Barcelona's coach (1988-1996), he was the ball that got things rolling.

Barcelona, which was always a good club team, benefited from Cruyff's influence as they were fine-tuned to be even better, and years down the road, Barcelona players—including Xavi, Iniesta, Pedro, Puyol, and others—made up the majority of Spain's national team, carrying forward the groundwork laid down by

Cruyff many years earlier. Without Cruyff's vision of the passing game, and, without the frequency with which it occurred under the guidance of Busquets, Xavi, Iniesta, and others, Spain likely would not have become the Golden Generation. Instead, they may have been like Spain of yore, a good team with winning results, without the right—for lack of a better word—"formula" to give them that extra push.

Essentially, before the World Cup of 2010, the 1964 and 2008 European Cup championships were Spain's big moments. The odd thing was, despite the lapse between 1964 and 2008, Spain had always been successful in most all competitions. It's not as if we're talking about a team like Nicaragua, one of the lower teams on the totem pole in CONCACAF, which is one of the weaker conferences on the totem pole of continental governing bodies. Spain was usually competing against top talent and performing well. Notably, from 1980 to 2000, Spain had a winning percentage that kept improving with time. But they couldn't win the World Cup.

Then, at last, Spain took the World Cup in 2010. Prior to South Africa, to the soccer world, Spain was regarded as one of the two best teams to never win the World Cup (the other being the Netherlands, who came close in the 70s led by Cruyff, Rinus Michels, and the idea of Total Football). It was a great achievement that was part of a long journey.

Currently, Spain might be caught in its familiar role of being a talented team that underachieves in World Cups. Russia 2018 will be an opportunity for the 2010 champs to prove otherwise.

ENGLAND

ENGLAND'S INTRIGUING DILEMMA

Of all the World Cup teams with a fascinating backstory, England's might win the prize. What might be most interesting of all is how developing teams can learn from England's long, illustrious history—one that is full of ups and downs.

People in England have been wondering when they're going to get back on track. Realistically, practically everyone from outside England has a strong opinion about what England's been doing wrong. Let's face it: England's good. People know it, yet they fail in the World Cup, and it's hard to figure out why. Some may argue they're stubborn and self-centered and only interested in their own ideas, while others say it's only bad luck; international soccer is a competitive sport, and it's only a matter of time before they become world champions again. However that conversation turns out, the fact remains: England hasn't won a World Cup since 1966.

To get England back on top, the common Englishman has reluctantly embraced outside views, including ideas from coaches Sven-Goran Eriksson and Frank Capello. And, more recently, they've looked within, hiring Gareth Southgate as their current coach. One field of thought is: The players are right, so it has to be a coaching issue. How much of England's problem has been coaching?

A HISTORICAL GLIMPSE AT ENGLISH COACHING

From the 1923 squad with players Henry Chambers, Bob Kelly, and Vic Watson, to the 1927 3-3 tie with Wales featuring Dixie

Dean's first game, to the 5-2 victory over Scotland in 1930 held at Wembley, to the 7-1 victorious thumping of the first ever match with Spain in 1931 led by Austen Campbell and Jack Smith, to the 1934 debut of Stanley Matthews against Wales in a 4-0 victory, to playing Italy in a contentious affair during 1934, to a 3-0 win over Germany in 1935, to the 1938 3-0 victory of England against the best of Europe (FIFA European Select), it's been a rich history of English soccer. England has long carried on the tradition of the game with passion, just as the game itself grew in popularity around the world during those years. Back in older times, based on their success and the limited amount of competition around the world, there was no reason to believe they were doing anything incorrectly.

The list of coaching is long, including from 1946 to today: Walter Winterbottom, Alf Ramsey, Joe Mercer, Don Revie, Ron Greenwood, Sir Bobby Robson, Graham Taylor, Terry Venables, Glenn Hoddle, Howard Wilkinson, Kevin Keegan, Peter Taylor, Sven-Goran Eriksson, Steve McClaren, Fabio Capello, Stuart Pearce, Roy Hodgson, Sam Allardyce, and the coach leading into Russia 2018, Gareth Southgate.

There was a time in 1960-1961, for example, under the guidance of coach Winterbottom, when England devastated opponents, which was not unusual. There was a 5-2 victory over Ireland on October 8, 1960, which extended into the following score lines: England 9, Luxembourg 0; England 4, Spain 2; England 5, Wales 1; England 9, Scotland 3; England 8, Mexico 0.

Of course, England would win the World Cup in 1966. From then, things weren't as kind in World Cup competitions. Call it a decline. Many people argue that England hasn't changed with the times. So what's the common thread in their approach?

From a coaching perspective, from the 1920s to now, it was a simplistic approach equaling cross after cross...after cross, with black high-top boots resembling a type of fashion choice that Morrissey could've worn in the mid-80s—minus the cleats, of course.

Fast forward fifty years: different equipment, similar approach, albeit with better technique, a quicker pace, and more skill. (And, of course, from time to time, a goal scored with ingenuity.)

Like England missing the 1930-1938 World Cups, could their decline from the good old days be an isolationist attitude carried over to coaching? Possibly. If so, while watching England in the World Cup, it's necessary to think of England's dilemma in terms of dribbling (which helps possession[37]), and the Clough factor.

DRIBBLING: WHERE ENGLAND CAN IMPROVE

From a nostalgic point of view, Stanley Matthews is regarded as England's greatest dribbler. For his time, he was quite revolutionary, moving past players with relative ease. It was a different era, that's for sure. By today's standards, he might be lucky to make his way onto a practice field. But some English folklore would lead you to believe his presence on the field was as if Messi and Denilson had a mythical child together. But he was very good. Just as Tom Finney was a good dribbler for 1952, and Matthews and Finney likely could have been good in 2002 (in the hypothetical time-traveling scenario that would allow players to adapt to the changing times).

But, the fact that England is struggling to move forward largely rests on their inability to encourage dribbling to the fresh young talent, who, instead, are being raised on ideologies based on a forgotten time when dribbling wasn't necessarily an advanced skill shared by all players, on all teams.

Aaron Lennon and Theo Walcott represent good dribblers held back from their true potential in the English system, which hasn't fully embraced dribbling as an art. In past years, the Garrinchas turned heads with exciting play, as do the Messis today. But the difference rests in the average player's ability to dribble better today than in the past—insofar as, the average players today reflect the dribbling ability of many top players from yesterday, such as Matthews and Finney. Confident dribblers can transcend the game in so many ways, which may be England's biggest challenge yet. Coaching can and should turn that misfortune around. But instead, England has been in a very interesting place.

Coaching has definitely had a lot to do with the overall theme to England's history with the game, and it will continue to play an important part in shaping their approach. Players alone can't change things or radically shift a style choice. It must first originate from those guiding them, those with the experience—the decision-makers.

As many coaches have come and gone, England has tried and failed, even going so far as to bring in help from Sweden and Italy. They even experimented with Stuart "Psycho" Pearce, the former outside defender who was part of the 1990 World Cup squad that made it to the semis, who was into punk rock. But, there's one man who never got the chance to "save England."

BRIAN CLOUGH: THE BEST COACH THAT NEVER WAS

Coaching England was an honor never given to Brian Clough, who, in his day, was widely agreed to be the best coach never to manage England. Of course, they've had many ostensibly distinguished choices for a coach to lead the country, including Hoddle, Eriksson, and Cappello. Though, referring to Eriksson as the coach, Clough quipped, "At last England have appointed a manager who speaks English better than the players." To miss out on the opportunity of having Clough as captain of the ship seemed odd, but conveniently prudent.

Clough was a former player with the national team, who jumped from his playing career—which he finished up in 1964 with Sunderland—to coaching Hartlepools United in 1965, beginning a rocky but successful career from the sidelines.

After leaving Derby County, and following his ambitious attempt to make Leeds *better* (not to mention the extremely popular TV debate with the former Leeds manager, Don Revie, that subsequently followed), he landed in Nottingham Forest, where he took their good but relatively average program to two consecutive European Club championships, which is unique to some of the elite clubs in Europe, including Bayern Munich, Liverpool, Ajax, Real Madrid, and AC Milan. Along the way, he told everyone in England, and whoever else was in earshot, how little they knew of the game.

He took pride in belittling all the directors and the decision-makers; in his eyes, doing the opposite of what they wanted logically propelled his coaching success in a positive direction. He needed someone to propel against. As he said, "Any idiot can coach a group of players to kick the ball as hard and high as possible and then gallop after it. Given time I could train a monkey to do it."[38] It was his unique insight into coaching that partly came from his disdain with the commonplace, boring ideas, and same old approach. He had that intangible quality that could feed players the right information they needed in order to perform in the right way, according to his vision (which may not have been in line with Pep Guardiola's tenure at Barcelona, but effective nonetheless).

For the most part, the people—or suspects—Clough put on his criticism list were the ones carrying around antiquated ideas that have kept England away from their true potential. And the potential's there. There's little doubting that. What Clough possessed was a keen sense of getting greatness out of individuals and how to put those individuals together into one cohesive group. As Clough said, "I'm not sure how important the formation is. What I do know is that players need to feel comfortable with the job you're asking them to carry out."[39] Easier said than done. Most coaches preach such a thing—a stump speech line for any coach trying to cover up for future losses on a score sheet and the inevitable meeting with the club owner.

However, in Clough's case, it seemed more action than talk. Roy Keane played for Clough, saying, "Brian Clough dealt in detail, facts, specific incidents, and invariably he got it right. Playing for him was demanding. I loved it."[40]

Aside from being the most likely foreign candidate to have replaced Rip Torn as Artie on *The Larry Sanders Show*,* with David Warner as a possible second, there were simple reasons that kept Clough away from the job as England's manager. He didn't respond well to authority; he was outspoken and blatantly challenged anyone in the public eye, criticizing practically everyone, including the people interviewing him. On coaching,

---

* Not to play second fiddle to Larry, of course, but to boss Hank around.

he said, "We can all talk a good game of football…But you've got to win something…Martin O'Neill for example. Martin talks superbly well. And played superbly well. He's now gone and won something. So he is now a football league manager. It's a hard job. It's a difficult job, especially when you're working for people who know nothing about football, that is directors."[41] Sounds a bit like Gene Hackman, taking over in *Hoosiers*. Similar to Hackman's character, who was forced to coach on the fringe of the basketball community in a small town, Clough did the best he could on the outskirts of Europe, making history with Nottingham Forest in 1979 and 1980. His attitude—which was unapologetic, ridiculing the decision-makers, calling attention to their lack of wisdom, at the behest of his own arrogance—was probably responsible for never attaining the position of head coach for England.

Could he have won the World Cup? Would his presence as coach (and the trickle-down effect to future generations) have left England in a better place today, with a better opportunity to win it all in Russia 2018?

This is part of England's mystery, struggle, and ongoing challenge. As to what could've happened if he had been the coach, we'll never know.

GETTING THINGS BACK ON TRACK

For the sake of their tradition, expectations, and potential, England's decision-makers are hopeful this trend of terrible, unfortunate, and unlucky World Cup performances and results won't go on in perpetuity. As of 2016, the FA—which formed in 1863, the first football association in the world—had placed their trust in the hands of technical director, Dan Ashworth.

The *Daily Mail*—a conservative British tabloid with a circulation of about two million—put out an article in 2016, delineating the plans of Ashworth and the FA to correct the past and prepare for the future. Without much detail, the article illuminated England's growing concern with improving their national team's standard of play as was indicated in the title of the article: "FA masterplan to win World Cup in 2022 includes hiring specialist coaches to help with possession and ball control," which was interesting, considering possession has proven to be a salient issue for the Three Lions.

Further concern was echoed from a piece in the *DailyMail.com*, February 18, 2016, by Charles Sale: "The FA's masterplan aimed at winning the World Cup in 2022 includes hiring an array of specialist coaches for when England have the ball, when they do not have the ball—and when they are kicking it. The FA are advertising on their website for national technical coaches, with the job descriptions saying: 'We are changing how we work, reallocating resources and investing heavily to create a team of exceptional people capable of creating winning England teams.'"

Without question, members of the FA are cognizant of the grave issues at hand, but a cynic would hasten to point out, it's not without superiority naivety. In typical fashion, they've conceded negligence on their part, pledging to fix it. However, their means of steering the ship in the right direction might have more to do with English pride than actually doing it right. By the FA's own concession, they intend to act on real change with English soccer, just as Napoleon promised the farm animals that things would change for the better. To some, it's nothing but old ideas disguised as new and improved action. Such critics are familiar with England as a steward of such promises in accordance with the underlining subtext: *We will change things. Change will come—as long as it follows closely in line with what we've already been doing.*

On the flipside, one could say they're on a progressive path to making their program better. The relationship with the FA and coaching is, and always will be, combined as one, so to speak, seeking to guide the team toward a better future.

And, as usual, notwithstanding past disappointment, England has every reason in the world to win the World Cup again. When that might be, is anyone's guess. After losing to Iceland in the 2016 European Cup, they have as good a chance of winning the World Cup in Russia as they would boarding a spaceship with Nick Pope on route to Andromeda. But, low and behold, after leading a strong World Cup qualification campaign, they're among the favorites in Russia.

They've had a profound influence on the game with their successful club teams and their consistent winning with the national team. Entering Russia 2018, the English are equipped with a phenomenal lineup, one they think has the potential to bring the trophy back to where they feel it belongs.

All of the history and all of the issues with England makes them one of the most exciting teams to watch.

ENGLAND'S INTERESTING APPROACH DOWN THE LINE

Part of England's approach to the game in general, which materializes in possession, is the need to possess the ball with purpose and to dominate the line with passes.

Typically, an English team will be seen making the same pass down the line between three players, essentially getting each player to practically the same position that the previous one was in. Depending on who you ask, it becomes clear that some parts of the field are more important than others. Having said that, critics would argue that the same pass down the line between three players takes England nowhere except down the line for the ongoing battle *of the line*.

Why is this the case? Why is the line so important? Possibly it's a choice of needing to be superior over narrow sections of real estate on the outskirts of land, fulfilling their inherent need to satisfy the classic colonial English quest for space and territory, not on the interior of a country but on the exterior, the coastal areas... India, South Africa, Hong Kong, and the Proclamation of 1763 in New England. (The British actually forbade the North American Colonies from going inland; i.e., "into the middle of the country,"[42] which was untamed wilderness. Of course, some British surveyors went into the interior of China and essentially said, "Egh. Yeah, I've seen enough." As it turns out, it's very hard to settle the interior of a country; England found they could use locals to work the interior—with things like hunting and gathering—while they'd oversee their affairs from the coast, controlling trade.)

Subsequently, trickling over to soccer, England has continued to battle with their opponent to own the areas around the line, which is tied to their exuberantly fervent need to cross the ball. In terms of the psychological parallels between colonial settlements of yore and the approach to soccer, the line represents the coastal area of a country, wherein the other side of the line represents the ocean; crossing the line means going into the ocean. They don't want to do that, considering soccer is a land battle and the areas outside of the lines are out of bounds. That's what the head coach is for; he rests offshore, with reinforcements, sending the occasional message to the players inland, with a flurry of hand gestures, some yelling, which is followed by resignation to the bench with his second-in-command, whispering over strategy, often by covering their mouths so no one can lip read.* Behind them are the common citizens, representing the homeland, telling the coaches what the players should do in language unfit for the queen. So it's as though, inherently, they must dominant the game as close to the "coastal region" of the field as possible. It's the English way, what else can you expect?

Establishing more of a "middle game" might be part of the plan administered by the current direction of the FA, which has openly been seeking a better way, and this is something to watch for in World Cup 2018.

Searching for improvements or not, England still provides an exciting presence in each game, playing with a quick pace and a lot of emotion. Despite the previous criticism, they will always be a threat to win the whole thing.

BRAZIL

BRAZIL LOOKING FOR WORLD CUP MAGIC AGAIN

Since winning their first World Cup in 1958, Brazil has been the standard. Over the years, teams like the upstart United States—in

---

* A practice done by many coaches as if the other team has installed a HAL 9000 on the other side of the field to decipher what they say and steal their strategy.

spite of their addled appreciation of the game—have looked to them for inspiration. However, it could be argued that, since 2010, and even 2006, with a recent decline in Brazilian soccer,* things haven't been looking so good for the leaders of the world's game. Who would've thought they would find themselves in such a predicament?

Winning the gold medal in the 2016 Olympics was definitely a step back in the right direction for Brazil. Dominating the South American qualification games for World Cup 2018 was also good news. But the criticism is still lingering, which has a lot to do with World Cups 2006, 2010, and 2014. There has been a lot of grumpiness regarding their style, and results, since the time Dunga took over as coach.

The argument could be made that Dunga, who was a good player, failed as a coach (particularly in 2010), inserting the wrong lineup and coaching them in a very straightforward fashion, thus hindering the classic stylistic Brazilian approach—one that was known for short passing, exuberant dribbling, flicks, and tricks. The lineup for World Cup 2010 was composed of bigger, gawky players, not the quintessential, creative Brazilian squad.

By the time Mano Menezes was released from his short stint as coach (2010-2012; in which he reintroduced a flashier style with players like Ganso, Neymar, and Pato), an old hand returned to lead the team. As Scolari reassumed the role of coach for Brazil he arguably brought back a boring style with the semifinal run in World Cup 2014 (which will always be remembered for the 7-1 loss to Germany), led by lackluster but steady players.

---

* A decline by Brazilian standards.

Then, in terms of disappointing Brazilian fans, Dunga did much of the same in the 2016 Copa America, as Brazil couldn't even get out of their group. That's worth repeating: Brazil couldn't even get out of their group. Without players like Ganso, Robinho, and Pato, Brazil lacked their traditional creative approach.

Everyone expects the Brazilians to lead the game, as they have consistently dominated the World Cup since 1958 with five titles. Sure, by their standards, they've had let downs, including 1974, 1978, 1982, 1986, 1990, 2006, 2010, and 2014, but they were always relevant, and some of those results ended in bad luck, which a team like England knows plenty about. Furthermore, those were let downs *for Brazil*. Any other upstart nation would have been very excited to trade places with Brazil in 1974 (where they placed fourth) and 1978 (where they placed third).

In years past, when defenses were less experienced and the globalization of soccer hadn't yet exploded as it has today, Brazil got away with possession with a purpose based on skillful play that was beyond most of their opponents. Teams were befuddled. Generally speaking, this was pre-1980s. Without the Internet, or widespread availability of TV,* each nation could still operate in isolation, so to speak, while maintaining a unique style. As the 1980s turned into the 90s and then the 2000s, players and coaches were dispersing around the globe with much more frequency, and

---

* Add to that VCRs. The availability of TV sets are one thing, but to study the games, any individual or group of coaches would have needed to record them. These conveniences were just that—conveniences for a select few. Unlike the modern era, the ability to study any team or player in great detail was much less widespread.

defenses gradually got better, so, as a result, Brazil was not such a surprise to opponents any more.

Unfortunately, for Brazilian fans who have studied the evolution of their team's superior World Cup history, of late, everything is forced and rushed and very "unBrazilian." Aside from the good Olympic run, which was largely an Under-23 team, Brazil has been *finding its way again* since 2010. They're uncharacteristically crossing the ball too often, while lacking classic dribblers with the swagger of Garrincha, the guile of Pele, the subtle nuance of Socrates, the showiness of Ronaldinho, and the excitement of Denilson. Neymar would naturally fill this role; however, there has been too much pressure on him to create everything in the attack, given that their creative central midfielders are not what they once were.*

Will they return to Brazil of old? What's gotten them in such a slump?

Some say it's the influence of Europe—too many players shuttling overseas at an early age and being overcoached within a structured passing system, which inevitably takes away their natural, creative Brazilian tendencies. Others believe the lineup has been all wrong. To them, if the lineup is right, it doesn't matter where the players land professionally.

With so many expectations to win, Brazil has neglected their focus on possession for possession's sake (with the classic

---

* Again, back to questionable Brazilian coaching decisions. While
Mano Menezes favored the style of play of Ganso, Scolari and Dunga
chose more defensive-minded midfielders.

futebol arte) and moved right into possession with a purpose; though they have always played with a free-flowing style, much of their possession since 2010 has been rushed, seeking scoring opportunities far too quickly in order to appease the pressure placed on them to accomplish amazing things every time they touch the ball. In fact, with those expectations looming large, their style has been hampered; players can't be expected to pull off highlight-type plays every time they get near the ball, but that is the common subtext with any Brazilian team. So instead of playing simple, you can discern from many players the thought of: *Now I have the ball, what amazing trick can I pull off?* But before they know it, their time has passed, and they distribute the ball. At the same time they were thinking of *something magnificent* they could've played the ball around simply—á la Spain—and eventually something incredible could've happened. With that said, Brazil finds a way to win.

Each World Cup, Brazil has the potential to be champions and to do it with amazing, creative ingenuity. Many Brazilians feel that Neymar and this team could be the group to bring home the trophy again.

NEYMAR LIVING UP TO PELE

Neymar, Brazil's answer to Garrincha and Pele with a modern twang, is carrying an entire nation's hopes and dreams into World Cup Russia.

Undoubtedly, any star Brazilian players will be compared with Pele, the best of them all. What can be written about him that hasn't already been said? He's one of the most celebrated athletes of all time. As a refresher…he was fast in longer sprints and quick in short spaces. He was effective with open-field dribbling and in crowded spaces. He could play long passes accurately, as well as short ones. He had every shot down. He was good with both feet. Despite being around five-foot-five, he was good in the air. And, yes, he scored a couple goals with the bicycle kick. He wasn't so much the maestro-in-the-middle type, building up the passing structure in possession, similar to Valderrama, Platini, or Hässler, but, similar to Messi, it seemed like everything he did was the right play for any given situation, be it a simple pass, making a teammate look good, or something amazing as in dribbling past three or four defenders with fake kicks, misdirection, and pure guile. In terms of dribbling, he wasn't as dynamic with the north-south savvy that Maradona had and was more of an east-west dribbler. (Though, Maradona had everything Pele did accept the aerial game.*)

After Pele, a long line of great Brazilian players followed, including: Zico, Socrates, Junior, Careca, Romario, Bebeto, Ronaldo, Rivaldo, Ronaldinho, Kaka, Robinho, and Neymar, to name a few.

For Russia 2018, Neymar, who came up with Santos and Robinho (Robinho, whose dribbling Pele liked so much), will have the responsibility of a nation to live up to Pele, along with everyone since, as well as carrying the nation one step closer to a sixth title.

---

* Maradona's one drawback was his lack of presence with head balls. Ranking Pele, Maradona, and Messi in the air would go like this (best to worst): Pele, Messi, Maradona. Though, it should go without saying, but said nonetheless, none of them were Oliver Bierhoff.

While Neymar has established himself as the heir apparent to Messi and Cristiano Ronaldo (as the world's next greatest player in the modern era) in terms of World Cups and in terms of how Brazilians view their great players, he'll be held up next to Garrincha and, of course, Pele, along with all the other salient talents that have adorned the Brazilian jersey. And, undoubtedly, he won't be considered equal to or greater than Pele without a World Cup title to his name. Not only that, he'll need to be a pivotal fixture in all Brazil's games (with goals and assists) on the march to a World Cup title for people to accept him as Pele's true successor. That's just part of the baggage that goes along with leading Brazil.

TOP 5 TEAMS OF WORLD CUP RUSSIA

(Based on recent records, FIFA rankings, star power, and style of play)

1. Germany

2. Brazil

3. Argentina

4. France

5. Spain

Of course, these five may not finish in this order based on many factors, including but not limited to group draws and elimination rounds (which, often, unfortunately pair two giants together right away; for example, England versus Germany in 2010 and France versus Italy in 1986).

TOP 10 PLAYERS OF WORLD CUP RUSSIA

(Based on overall offensive contribution to the field of play)

1. Messi (Argentina)

Messi is like the string in string theory. There are the electrons, which are the fans. There are the protons and neutrons, which are the coaches and Argentine Football Association. There are the quarks, which are the players on the current squad, stars, and supporting cast. Then, there is the string, the one that pushes them all, Messi.

2. Neymar (Brazil)

Neymar representing Brazil, ditto.

3. C. Ronaldo (Portugal)

C. Ronaldo representing Portugal, ditto.

The rest of these guys are like really good quarks.

4. Hazard (Belgium)

5. Griezmann (France)

6. Kroos (Germany)

7. Suarez (Uruguay)

8. James (Colombia)

9. Di Maria (Argentina)

10. Herrera* (Mexico)

Second Team: Müller (Germany), Corona (Mexico), Payet (France), Rooney (England), Isco (Spain), Falcao (Colombia), Willian (Brazil), Özil (Germany), Salah (Egypt), and Kagawa (Japan).

---

* It can be successfully argued that James and Falcao of Colombia (and even Corona of Mexico) are better individual talents than Herrera, but they are not better organizational passers, which is what this list needed. Not a big goal-scorer, Herrera does all the brilliant subtle things that make his team tick.

COMEBACK TEAMS
FOR WORLD CUP 2022

Italy, the United States, the Netherlands, and Chile

ITALY

A BRIEF TEAM HISTORY

World Cup titles: 4 (1934, 1938, 1982, 2006)

Referring to the Bayern Munich coach, Carlo Ancelotti, Paul Breitner said, "He's an Italian, and Italians were born for not losing."[43] Unfortunately for Italy, in the 2017 World Cup qualification playoff with Sweden, this was not the case, as they were outdone by one goal. And they would not make the trip to Russia 2018. The last time Italy missed a World Cup was in 1958. As one of the leaders in the game, the illustrious Italians are certain, if not destined, to turn things around come 2022.

The United States, the Netherlands, and Chile deserve an in-depth look as they got unlucky in the 2018 World Cup qualifications, and they should definitely make a comeback for World Cup 2022.

UNITED STATES

A BRIEF TEAM HISTORY

The United States got third place at the first World Cup in 1930. Then, in 1934, they made it no farther than the first round. They didn't compete in 1938. In 1950, at the World Cup in Brazil, they lost out in the group phase; though, they had a historical victory over England. From that point on, they didn't qualify for the next forty years.

Italy 1990 would be their grand reentry into the World Cup, thanks to a miraculous long-distance volley in qualifications by UCLA's Paul Caligiuri against Trinidad and Tobago, on the road, in a must-win game. Despite putting up a valiant effort, the US left Italy early, unable to escape their group.

As hosts in 1994, led on the backline by Alexi Lalas, the US made a strong push into the second round, losing in a low-scoring thriller to the eventual champs, Brazil, on a goal by Bebeto. Although the US qualified for 1998, it wasn't the best showing, as they failed to get out of their group.

World Cup 2002 offered a bit more promise as the US had a decent result in the group, advancing to the second round where they met an old foe, Mexico, winning 2-0 with goals from McBride and Donovan. This led to a huge showdown in the quarterfinals with Germany, which resulted in a loss. At Germany in the 2006 World Cup, the US failed to get out of their group, ending the tournament in disappointment.

Seeking a new direction, coach Bob Bradley replaced Bruce Arena for World Cup 2010, which saw the introduction of Michael Bradley and Jozy Altidore. The US had a big win over Algeria, thanks to a goal from Landon Donovan, which led to a first-place ranking in their group ahead of England. The second round wasn't so kind, as Ghana escaped with a victory.

As of 2014, under coach Klinsmann—who had said there was no way his team would conceivably win the World Cup that year— the US achieved some respect by making it to the round of 16, but lost to a talented Belgian side.

CONCACAF COMPETITIONS

The United States has had good success in the CONCACAF Gold Cup, winning in 1991, 2002, 2005, 2007, 2013, and 2017.

FACTS ABOUT THEIR COUNTRY

The United States has a population of a little over 324.7 million people, with an estimated GDP of around 18.5 trillion, often first in the world.

When it comes to sports, the US is often united on all fronts, as a leader in practically every competition, particularly with the

Olympics. Traditionally, the most popular sports have been the Big Three: baseball, basketball, and football. Over the years, soccer has pushed its way into the fourth spot, jostling with hockey and tennis.* Soccer is unquestionably growing more popular each year, which has many teams around the world concerned that someday very soon the US will also come to dominate it.

Clint Dempsey—the Texas native, the high-scoring phenom, the aspiring rapper, the fisherman—has stepped to the top of the list for the most goals in US soccer history, alongside another big goal-scorer, Landon Donovan (who finished his career with 57). Cobi Jones has the most caps with 164.

Many different beers fill up the bars when the US plays games on TV. Some of those include Budweiser, Miller, and Coors, along with many microbrews from coast to coast.

WHERE THE TEAM IS TODAY—TACTICS AND STRATEGIES

Under coach Klinsmann, the US tinkered with lineups. Under Arena 2.0, they essentially went with a 4-4-2.

The amazing potential of the USMNT will be on full display as World Cup 2022 approaches. The style of American soccer is full of energy with a touch of patience. Past players on the USMNT were great athletes, but they lacked (the all-important)

---

* Among other sports, like track and field and golf. Prior to the 1980s, for many years, bowling was the most popular sport on TV.

patience and structure in possession. It was simply "the way" of American soccer back in the pre-2000s era. Much of America's "on the go culture" has been reflected in teams of the past. They would punch the ball forward, quickly attempting chances at goal. After all, traditional American sports fans "want big scores." This, in part, caused past teams to rush things...always seeking that immediate goal, trading punches with opponents, and often becoming overwhelmingly bewildered by the powers of possession from masterful teams from Europe and South America.

As the years have gone by, the American team has slightly adjusted to becoming more thoughtful with a slower approach, using possession to their advantage. Today they reflect less of an American team of the past and more of a fledgling Dutch outfit, albeit with a heavy dose of England. Regardless, much of this shift has to do with the establishment of the MLS in 1995. Its creation has allowed US players to compete domestically in a viable outdoor league, which has seasoned them to the ways and means of top talent from around the world. And thus: advantage US.

ARENA, BRADLEY, KLINSMANN, AND SARACHAN—A BRIEF COACHING PORTRAIT

Bruce Arena made his second stop as coach of the USMNT during the 2018 World Cup qualification campaign.

Arena has been known as a good organizer and communicator. The players have always seemed to know their place on his teams in a good way. With few exceptions, he preferred a large backline and bigger players with a strong presence on the field. The interesting thing about Arena is that he has always done very well in domestic competitions. That is, when all the teams are playing the same style (essentially getting the ball down the line and into the box*), his teams have usually come out ahead. However, his approach—including lineup choices and style of play—has met a tough audience outside of CONCACAF in the 2002 and 2006 World Cups, where the style of play was a bit different. Leading up to those campaigns, winning was something Arena was used to.

As a player, Arena was a goalie (and even played one game with the US national team), and then as coach of Virginia University he won four consecutive NCAA national titles. As coach in the MLS, he's won five MLS Cups (two with DC United and three with LA Galaxy). He first coached the USMNT from 1998-2006 after replacing Steve Sampson, wherein Arena led the charge in the 2002 and 2006 World Cups, along with a few Gold Cup titles.

Following the 2006 World Cup, Bob Bradley took over and coached during the 2010 World Cup. Bradley was replaced by Jurgen Klinsmann, who coached during the 2014 World Cup, and he was in turn replaced by Bruce Arena. For his second run at coaching the USMNT, Arena inherited a team in flux.

Jurgen Klinsmann had coached the team to mixed results, albeit a winning record. By the time Klinsmann and the USMNT lost 4-0 to Costa Rica (in 2016), Sunil Gulati—the US Soccer president—

---

* A simplification, though, people within the American soccer community, including Alexi Lalas, have pointed out that Arena is not the biggest Xs and Os coach around.

cleaned house, rehiring Arena. All of this was smack in the middle of World Cup qualifications.

With some bad luck, the USMNT met a tough opponent in their final World Cup qualification game, losing to Trinidad and Tobago in October of 2017. For the first time since 1986, the US would not qualify for the World Cup.

Following the loss, Arena resigned as coach. The interim coach who took his place was the experienced Dave Sarachan, a former player and coach at Cornell University, who also played and coached professionally, who also happened to be a longtime associate of Arena.

The next US coach, whoever that may be, has a fresh group of talent to lead the team into World Cup 2022.

KEY PLAYERS AND THEIR CHARACTERISTICS

Christian Pulisic and Darlington Nagbe

Christian Pulisic is a system-oriented midfielder, which is just what American soccer needs. Brand new to the scene, a guy who seems like he'd be really good at Lumosity, Pulisic has made a great impression with his simple, technically sound style of play (a style that leads to more scoring opportunities), which has earned him playing time with Borussia Dortmund. He's not a dazzling technically sound dribbler—like Denilson from Brazilian days of old—but an effective one, using his body well in tight spaces, which opens up situations for smart passes.

Darlington Nagbe, son of Joe Nagbe (a soccer player from Liberia), has stepped up as one of the best center midfielders in CONCACAF, alongside Herrera from Mexico. Under the coaching guidance of Caleb Porter, Nagbe has won the NCAA Championship with the University of Akron (Ohio) and the MLS Cup with the Portland Timbers. He's a talented player, equipped with elusive dribbling and masterful passing, who, in a subtle way, moves around the field like the queen on a chessboard directed by Kasparov. His all-around touch and knowledge of the game are reminiscent of Chad Deering, but Nagbe doesn't have quite the arrogant on-field presence as Deering did. Nagbe's very mechanical; he's very robotic in an elegant way. With him on the field, possession soccer is in good hands.

KEY PLAYER STATS

	Games Played	Goals	Scoring Percentage
Christian Pulisic	20	9	45%
Darlington Nagbe	24	1	4%

WHAT TO WATCH FOR ON TV—HOW MESSI, NEYMAR, KROOS, AND OTHERS PLAY

As part of the new wave of American soccer talent, younger players like Nagbe and Pulisic are paving the way for great things to come. They've had past help from Dempsey, Donovan, and Ramos, and the road to greatness continues, as the USMNT is becoming increasingly more technically sound in its approach.

More and more, the US team is using a thoughtful, structured approach to passing which is occurring at a greater frequency than in previous generations. They'll apply this technique, attempting to keep the ball away from opponents, which helps the US a great deal on the defensive end. It also increases the United States' scoring chances as confidence builds throughout a game. Essentially, all the "confidence" that Klinsmann stressed as being so important will filter into the team's progression down the line.

Prior to Arena's first quest as coach, Steve Sampson, and others, simply wanted the US to have a good showing. Arena and Bradley, to their credit, pushed the idea of winning the whole thing. Despite knowing it would be a challenge, deep down, they really thought it was possible. Then Klinsmann famously asserted just prior to World Cup 2014 that there was no way the USMNT was going to win that tournament. His attitude was *let's just have a good showing, guys*, which put the US back a few years. Now, following a hard-fought 2018 qualification run, the US is shifting gears and preparing for 2022.

Overall Team Rating: 7.7, leaning toward 7.5

Right now, the US is struggling to find its correct lineup while coming off a tumultuous coaching change from Klinsmann to Arena 2.0. With the right lineup, the US is a team easily in the low 8 range.

THE NETHERLANDS

A BRIEF TEAM HISTORY

The Netherlands has provided one of the best programs in world soccer history. Though, by no fault of their own, or *completely* by fault of their own, they've had a hit or miss relationship with the World Cup.

In 1930, they didn't compete in the World Cup. In 1934 and 1938, they didn't get past the first round. From 1950 to 1970, they didn't compete. Then, out of nowhere, came the "Total Football" teams of the 70s. In World Cups 1974 and 1978, they took second place, losing first in '74 to West Germany and in '78 to Argentina. Things went downhill from there, as they didn't qualify in 1982 and 1986.

After they won the European Cup in 1988, things improved on the World Cup front as they reached the round of 16 in 1990, then the quarterfinals in 1994, eventually taking fourth place in 1998. But, 2002 was a time of transition, as they didn't qualify for Korea-Japan. They were back in the mix in 2006, reaching the round of 16, losing 1-0 to Portugal.

In South Africa, they had a great team, and it came down to the Netherlands and Spain in the final: The two best teams never to win a World Cup. The Dutch versus Spain (who inherited Dutch training techniques); so essentially, the Dutch versus the Dutch. No matter what, there would be a new World Cup champion in 2010. Yet, the real Netherlands strayed away from their go-to game of passing, instead favoring a rough-and-tumble approach, trying to knock Spain off their game, literally. In the end, the Spanish got a goal from Iniesta late in the game, giving the Netherlands another disappointing second-place finish.

At Brazil in 2014, the Netherlands did well, earning third place. They started out with a bang, demolishing Spain in a rematch 5-1; then they beat Australia 3-2; and finally they knocked off Chile 2-0, earning first place in their group, which sent Spain home early. In the second round, they beat Mexico 2-1, which led to the quarterfinals where they bested Costa Rica in penalty kicks. More penalty kicks came in the semis, where they lost to a determined and talented Argentinean side. Following that, in the consolation match, they defeated the hosts, Brazil by a score of 3-0 with goals from Robin van Persie, Daley Blind, and Georginio Wijnaldum. As the 2018 World Cup qualifications finished, the Netherlands found themselves out of luck.

EUROPEAN CUP

Led by Ruud Gullit and Marco van Basten, the Netherlands had a big year in 1988, winning the European Cup for the first time. It was a brilliant tournament for the Dutch, showing how dynamic their brand of soccer can be.

FACTS ABOUT THEIR COUNTRY

The Netherlands is a classical maritime nation also well-known for dairy products. They have a population of around 17 million people, and a GDP of approximately 769 billion.

Their most capped goalie is Edwin van der Sar with 130. Who is the oldest Dutch player to make a debut performance for his country? The 39-year-old goalie, Sander Boschker, who played his one and only game in 2010 against Ghana.

There are many Dutch beers to choose from, including Heineken (founded circa 1873) and Amstel (founded in 1870), which are in abundance as fans watch their team on TV.

WHERE THE TEAM IS TODAY—TACTICS AND STRATEGIES

Whether going with a 4-2-3-1, 4-4-2, 4-3-3, or some variation in between, the Netherlands will string together brilliant team play. With a strong culture of success, combined with clinical team passing along with magical individual talent, the Dutch are keen on getting big results, confident they have the players to push them over the top as 2022 comes around.

DANNY BLIND—A BRIEF COACHING PORTRAIT

Danny Blind took over the Dutch coaching job in 2015, after having previously coached with Ajax and with the Netherlands as an assistant.

During the qualification run of World Cup 2018, Coach Blind had the Netherlands in their typical passing scheme, working the ball across the field and into formidable positions down the pitch to allow the players more touches on the ball than their opponent, which is part of the classical Dutch "thinking" approach. Whoever takes on the coaching responsibility in the near future, this approach will likely remain the same for the Dutch.

KEY PLAYERS AND THEIR CHARACTERISTICS

Arjen Robben, Georginio Wijnaldum, and Jeremain Lens

Arjen Robben is a dazzling attacking player usually found on the wing using his speed and remarkable dribbling ability. He can take the ball down the wing or cut back inside better than most players who've ever played the position. He's always a threat. Considering his age, he may not be around in 2022, though his legacy out wide will remain.

Georginio Wijnaldum, a central midfielder who has bounced around from Dutch and English teams, brings passing connectivity in the midfield, along with tough grit and goal-scoring touch around the box.

Jeremain Lens is a forward with over 30 caps. Whether it's dribbling past a goalie and scoring on an empty net with the outside of his foot from near the corner flag or side-stepping a defender and blasting the ball into the net, it would appear that any team with Lens on the field will increase their chances to score. He has magical skill and comes across as a mix between Landon Donovan and Clint Dempsey.

KEY PLAYER STATS

	Games Played	Goals	Scoring Percentage
Robben	96	37	38%
Wijnaldum	42	8	19%
Lens	34	8	23%

WHAT TO WATCH FOR ON TV—HOW MESSI, NEYMAR, KROOS, AND OTHERS PLAY

For anyone new to soccer: The Dutch are passing masters. Their technique, vision, accuracy, placement, and timing are the standard for any young player looking for guidance. They also combine a sound passing structure with immaculate individual talent, using the dribble to keep opponents off balance. They bring a rich tradition of high-quality soccer, and as a result (which aficionados of the game know all too well), they're still the best team never to win the World Cup. As World Cup 2022 draws closer, the Dutch will be ready to seize the title, once and for all.

Overall Team Rating: 8

CHILE

A BRIEF TEAM HISTORY

Following two wins and a loss, Chile didn't get out of group play in the 1930 World Cup. Instead, their neighbor, Argentina, advanced onward. They didn't compete in 1934 and 1938.

World Cup 1950—held in Brazil—was another disappointment for the Chileans. Despite having a win over the United States, they couldn't get out of their group, with two losses to England and Spain. For 1954 and 1958, they did not competeAs hosts in 1962, Chile finally got out of group play with two wins against Switzerland and Italy and a loss to West Germany. In the quarterfinals, they defeated the Soviet Union. They lost to Brazil in the semifinals, eventually placing third overall with a 1-0 win over Yugoslavia in the consolation match.

In 1966, they placed last in their group, losing to Italy, tying North Korea, then losing to the Soviet Union. Chile didn't compete in 1970. World Cup 1974 wasn't much better, as they didn't advance from their group with two ties and a loss. They didn't compete in 1978.

In 1982, they finished last in their group with three losses to Austria, West Germany, and Algeria. They didn't qualify in 1986, 1990, and 1994—not good years for Chile. In 1998, they got second place in their group by tying Italy, Austria, and Cameroon. But, despite a goal from Salas, they lost right away in the round of 16 to Brazil.

In 2002 and 2006, they didn't compete. In 2010, with $32.95 million going to the winning team, Chile placed second in their group, advancing to the round of 16 where they were eliminated by Brazil. At World Cup 2014 in Brazil, Chile placed second in their group (as they had in 1998 and 2010), but lost to Brazil, yet again, in the round of 16.

What an interesting turn of events for Chile: In their last three World Cup appearances—1998, 2010, and 2014—they lost in the second round to Brazil after placing second in their group. During the South American 2018 World Cup qualification campaign, Chile was knocking on the door of Russia until Peru made a last-minute run.

SOUTH AMERICAN COMPETITIONS

Since 1916, the Copa America (previously called the South American Championship) has presented a challenge to Chile. Most championships have gone to Uruguay, Argentina, and Brazil whereas Chile has won only two titles in 2015 and 2016. A long time to wait for South American glory, but they did it with an extremely talented group of players.

Chile was running full throttle in 2016 with a devastatingly creative side as they defeated Argentina in the finals of the Copa

America, hinting at things to come for the World Cup in Russia. But, things weren't meant to be, and they'll have their sights on the 2022 World Cup.

As of 2017, Chile placed second in the Confederations Cup held in Russia.

FACTS ABOUT THEIR COUNTRY

Chile, the land of great wine, has a population of around 18 million, and a GDP of approximately 297 billion.

Claudio Bravo, the Chilean keeper, won the Golden Glove award at the 2017 Confederations Cup. It's not just fine wines that Chile produces and exports all over the world, there's also something brewing with their soccer program. And soccer's the most popular sport in Chile. But, when it comes to drinks, many fans watching Chile on TV might be enjoying a variety of wines, including San Pedro or Lapostolle, or, possibly, popular Chilean beers from the Barrilito beer shop.

WHERE THE TEAM IS TODAY—TACTICS AND STRATEGIES

As far as World Cups go, maybe they haven't had the most lucrative past, but the recent Copa America champs are a lethal force to reckon with. Defensively, they're a forest of quickness. They swarm their opponents. With Vidal's leadership in the middle and a strong backline, they're a tough team to break down.

They exude offensive flair and creative ingenuity like any other great team in the past. Their passes flow from skillful interplay and quick, tenacious, attacking players with an eye for goal. While they'll probably be in a 4-4-2, they seem to do everything right, and they're expecting big things going into World Cup 2022.

JUAN ANTONIO PIZZI AND REINALDO RUEDA—A BRIEF COACHING PORTRAIT

Juan Antonio Pizzi is a former forward who played professionally from 1987-2002 with a variety of teams, including Barcelona and River Plate. He was born in Argentina but played with the Spanish national team in the 1990s.

He took over the Chilean team in 2016. In doing so, Chile has adopted a fluent style, relying on smaller players that exude quickness and craft on the ball. The current team led by the veterans Sanchez and Vidal resembles a mix between Spain and Argentina at their very best, which includes the structured passing of Spain and the exuberant talent on the ball of Argentina. Considering his background, this might just be the perfect generation of Chilean players to compliment the vision of Coach Pizzi. Pizzi was replaced by Reinaldo Rueda, who was born in Colombia and brings a lot of coaching experience. Whoever the coach ends up being for the 2022 campaign, Chile is on the right path to success.

KEY PLAYERS AND THEIR CHARACTERISTICS

Alexis Sanchez, Arturo Vidal, and Eduardo Vargas

Alexis Sanchez is a very talented forward with past experience at Barcelona. He helped lead Chile to the impressive 2016 Copa America championship. He's very crafty on the ball in tight situations around the box (some of this skill was fine-tuned at Barcelona), with good quickness and a knack for finding teammates with great passes.

Arturo Vidal—who plays professionally with Bayern Munich—is the extraordinary center midfielder who keeps everything in check for Chile with defensive responsibilities and organization. As far as finding the right offensive rhythm for each given moment, be it a pass or dribble, Vidal is one of a kind. His passes constantly showcase smart distribution of the ball and high-quality touch. He's one of the premier center midfielders in the game today.

Eduardo Vargas is a great forward with quickness and speed who orbits around his teammate Alexis Sanchez, making creative passes that have direction that constantly press an opposing team. If Vargas, Vidal, and Sanchez can stay healthy, Chile is in good hands as they approach World Cup 2022.

KEY PLAYER STATS

	Games Played	Goals	Scoring Percentage
Alexis Sanchez	119	39	32%
Arturo Vidal	97	23	23%
Eduardo Vargas	80	35	43%

WHAT TO WATCH FOR ON TV—HOW MESSI, NEYMAR, KROOS, AND OTHERS PLAY

Despite having trouble in the South American 2018 World Cup campaign, as things stand, there are very few teams like Chile. They're high on confidence from a back-to-back championship run at the Copa America (2015 and 2016), but they'll need to do some regrouping as they prepare for 2022. Are they running out of steam from 2015 and 2016? Possibly. But they still have key players in place.

Keep an eye on the obvious: An avalanche of an attack from very quick players that collectively feed off one another. When they're on, which is often, everything clicks with this group. They've got the magic touch, counterattacking to great effect while out-possessing opponents with aesthetic authority. Quite simply, they're a thrill to watch. And they should be back with a vengeance in 2022.

Overall Team Rating: 9.5

After the 2015 and 2016 Copa America titles, Chile was looking like a solid 10. With some bad luck in the South American World Cup qualifications, they're currently more like a 9.5—a 9.5 that met tough resistance in the ever-competitive forest of South American teams.

AUTHOR'S NOTE

All information in this book is current at the time the book was published. Sometimes, teams change at the last minute or even during the World Cup. For example, during the 1982 World Cup, a French player was sent home for having an affair with Platini's wife and then brought back. In the 2010 World Cup, within the camp of a different French squad, there was a team protest against the coaching staff for a fellow player being sent home. That's just how the World Cup goes sometimes. With that said, every effort was made to keep the information in this book as up to date as possible.

All formations—for all teams—are subject to change based a number of factors revolving around coaching decisions that usually include team chemistry, player suspensions, player performance, issues with another team, and injuries. Having said that, most teams stay with the same formation, but, up to the last minute prior to a game, a coach may change things up.

Each team's "Overall Team Rating" is on a scale of 10, like in gymnastics. Each team's rating (or score) is based on a number of factors, including as much of the following as possible: The team's FIFA ranking (as of late 2017), recent record (which includes the past two World Cups, smaller tournaments, and friendlies), historical results,* star players, style of a play, chemistry between players, and a good old-fashioned hunch.

For certain endnotes that include "circa" with an accessed date, the circa in question refers to around two months prior to that accessed date.

---

* This one is tricky, as the matter of past teams endowing their qualities to new generations of players is in part due to coaching, but it also potentially gets muddled in pseudo-science, yet many teams follow the same trends that were established by their predecessors many years ago.

ENDNOTES & CITATIONS

1. Many people feel the European Cup is more competitive than the World Cup. After all, it is widely regarded that Europe has the best national teams and more countries with high-quality soccer experience competing for the title than, say, the South American Cup, with less nations, allowing Brazil and Argentina to battle it out, along with Uruguay and Chile, to a lesser extent. Within Europe, the competition is fierce, including England, Germany, France, the Netherlands, Denmark, Czechoslovakia, Russia, Italy, and Spain, along with other teams, including Poland, Greece, Bulgaria, Romania, Switzerland, Austria, Hungary, Sweden, the Ukraine, Scotland, Ireland, and Northern Ireland.

   With the World Cup, it can be argued that "less talented" nations take up positions that more experienced European teams would have otherwise taken. Traditionally, teams from North America, Africa, and Asia just haven't been as good as European teams, as shown by World Cup records. So for Germany to excel in the European Cup is more evidence of their overall dominance in world soccer.

2. The GDP for all nations within reflects the totals from the GDP nominal and not the GDP PPP (Purchasing Power Parity). All estimates are approximate.

3. Miguel Angel Violan, *Pep Guardiola: The Philosophy That Changed The Game* (Germany: Meyer and Meyer Sport, 2014), 49.

4. Spain unequivocally proved that the two-man game, otherwise known as Tiki-Taka, works. Some of the people who got tired of it were essentially fed up with Spain's predictable success.

It's arguably the best method for team passing ever adapted. Based on two counts it works better than anything ever thrown on a field. Count one: The record speaks for itself. Spain's unparalleled success with the 2008 European Championship, the 2010 World Cup Championship, and the 2012 European Championship shows that it works. It's almost impossible to argue with that. Count two: It's aesthetically pleasing. Some may disagree, but in the absence of Tiki-Taka—regardless of what era the game is from—there are blatantly painful gaps in possession that call out for one thing: "More Spain! Less of whatever these two teams are trying to do!" Spain's constant passing connections made it "the game" to watch, and, knowing the standard they created made it hard to watch anything else.

Many naysayers claim Tiki-Taka was, is, and always will be, boring and uncreative. The juxtaposition to this claim is that Spain's short passes were a sign of mental creativity. You could just as easily argue that not playing Tiki-Taka is in and of itself "boring and uncreative."

Led by Puyol, Pique, Busquets, Xavi, Iniesta, Alonso, Silva, Pedro, and others, the Golden Generation, as they're known, brought about historical success with the Tiki-Taka approach. It will be virtually impossible for future Spanish teams to live up to the Golden Generation. However, they carry with them a unique short passing style, which, like it or not, has produced great success.

5. Without the right players conducting the Tiki-Taka model, in the right way, which is all about patience and timing, Spain might

not get the best scoring chances around goal. The players must have the patience, knowledge, experience, and the ability to make ostensibly "boring passes," which appear to be going nowhere, turn into scoring opportunities. It's a lot to ask. As Spain's Golden Generation is slowly beginning to drift away into retirement, this is a concern for coach Julen Lopetegui.

6. Christina Settimi, "The World's Highest-Paid Soccer Players 2017: Cristiano Ronaldo, Lionel Messi Lead The List," *Forbes*, published May 26, 2017, accessed June 11, 2017, https://www.forbes.com/pictures/5924841ba7ea434078d44dcf/1-cristiano-ronaldo-real-/#37db0e7f730a.

7. *Wikipedia, The Free Encyclopedia*, s.vv. "Josef Hugi (5 World Cup goals)," (accessed circa April 29, 2017), https://en.wikipedia.org/wiki/Switzerland_at_the_FIFA_World_Cup#Top_goalscorers.

8. *Wikipedia, The Free Encyclopedia*, s.vv. "Josef Hugi (6 World Cup goals)," (accessed circa April 29, 2017), https://en.wikipedia.org/wiki/1954_FIFA_World_Cup.

9. FIFA.com, s.vv. "Josef Hugi, Top 100 Goalscorers," (accessed September 9, 2017) http://www.fifa.com/worldcup/news/y=1998/m=7/news=top-100-goalscorers-71759.html.

10. There are a lot of complete players who are very good talents, but not great, or as they say, superstar caliber. Clint Dempsey, for example, in his prime, was an outstanding player with one drawback: He was never outright fast. The same can be said for John Barnes and Cuauhtemoc Blanco. In their prime, Pele, Maradona, and Messi had speed that set them apart from the fastest players on the field, which helped define them as complete players.

11. Quote accessed via Facebook correspondence with Mohamad Al-Bacha on September 14, 2017, Central Standard Time (Chicago, Illinois).

12. "1994 FIFA World Cup USA," FIFA.com, accessed June 17, 2017, https://www.fifa.com/worldcup/archive/usa1994/index.html.

13. "2014 FIFA World Cup Brazil in numbers," FIFA.com, accessed June 17, 2017, http://www.fifa.com/worldcup/news/y=2014/m=9/news=2014-fifa-world-cup-braziltm-in-numbers-2443025.html.

14. "2014 FIFA World Cup Brazil," FIFA.com, accessed June 18, 2017, http://www.fifa.com/worldcup/archive/brazil2014/index.html.

15. "2014 FIFA World Cup Brazil in numbers," FIFA.com, accessed June 18, 2017, http://www.fifa.com/worldcup/news/y=2014/m=9/news=2014-fifa-world-cup-braziltm-in-numbers-2443025.html.

16. *Wikipedia, The Free Encyclopedia*, s.vv. "Swiss Laboratory for Doping Analyses 2014 World Cup," (accessed circa October 7, 2017), https://en.wikipedia.org/wiki/Swiss_Laboratory_for_Doping_Analyses.

17. Ian O'Riordan, "Doping controls at the World Cup in Brazil leave a lot to be desired," *The Irish Times*, published June 7, 2014, accessed February 13, 2017, http://www.irishtimes.com/sport/other-sports/doping-controls-at-the-world-cup-in-brazil-leave-a-lot-to-be-desired-1.1823913.

18. "How to Kick a Goal-Scoring World Cup Corner Kick," *Bloomberg*, accessed circa June 14, 2017, http://www.bloomberg.com/news/videos/b/d473ce8b-298d-4155-afe2-28eda40e8314.

19. Michael Caley, "Why have so many goals been scored off corner kicks at the World Cup?" *The Washington Post*, published June 24, 2014, accessed circa June 6, 2017, https://www.washingtonpost.com/news/fancy-stats/wp/2014/06/24/why-have-so-many-goals-been-scored-off-corner-kicks-at-the-world-cup/?utm_term=.f5724a4d4c54.

20. UEFA is a well-known organization that, at times, seems to overlap FIFA events. UEFA works with FIFA on many matters, but they are a continental confederation, like CONCACAF. UEFA, or the Union of European Football Associations, was founded in 1954 in Switzerland, and it represents the national football associations of Europe. UEFA oversees national and club competitions, including the UEFA European Championship, UEFA Champions League, UEFA Europa League, and UEFA Super Cup.

21. Azerbaijan, Georgia, Kazakhstan, Russia, and Turkey are UEFA members, despite the majority of their geographical territory being outside of continental Europe.

22. French Guiana, Guyana, and Suriname are CONCACAF members, although they are in South America. The French Guiana team is a member of CONCACAF but not of FIFA.

23. *Wikipedia, The Free Encyclopedia*, s.vv. "List of films considered the worst," (accessed June 4, 2017), https://en.wikipedia.org/wiki/List_of_films_considered_the_worst.

24. ESPN might as well change their name to NSN, "No Soccer Network."

25. *Wikipedia, The Free Encyclopedia*, s.vv. "CONCACAF Leadership," (accessed June 6, 2017), https://en.wikipedia.org/wiki/CONCACAF#Leadership

26. Stadium capacities were gathered from Wikipedia.

27. *Wikipedia, The Free Encyclopedia*, s.vv. "VEB Arena," (accessed May 18, 2017), https://en.wikipedia.org/wiki/VEB_Arena

28. Vladimir II Monomakh (1053-1125) was a grand prince of Kievan Rus', with ties to the Rurik Dynasty (which was founded by the Varangian, or "Viking," Rurik in 862 AD, who established a base in Novgorod).

29. Oleg Svyatoslavich (1052-1115), a cousin and enemy of Vladimir II Monomakh, was a prince associated with the Rurik Dynasty.

30. Alexander Nevsky (1221-1263) was a key figure in Russian history; a prince of Novgorod, Kiev, and Vladimir, famous for winning battles over German and Swedish forces, including the "Battle on the Ice" in 1242 AD, between Novgorod forces led by Nevsky and the German Teutonic Knights, on Lake Peipusk, which lies between modern-day Estonia and Russia; Nevsky also guided treaties with the Golden Horde in the south.

31. *Wikipedia, The Free Encyclopedia*, s.v. "Scythia," (accessed April 12, 2017), https://en.wikipedia.org/wiki/Scythia.

32. *Wikipedia, The Free Encyclopedia*, s.vv. "Europe's Most Dangerous City," (accessed April 12, 2017), https://en.wikipedia.org/wiki/Rostov-on-Don.

33. Gilbert, Simon, & Walker, Marc, "Coventry named seventh most dangerous city in Europe – and the worst in Britain," *Mirror Online*, published January 5, 2017, accessed April 12, 2017, http://www.mirror.co.uk/news/uk-news/coventry-named-seventh-most-dangerous-9568642.

34. Simon Gilbert, "Coventry named most dangerous city in UK – and in Europe's top 10," *Coventry Telegraph*, published January 5, 2017 (updated January 6, 2017), accessed April 12, 2017, http://www.coventry telegraph.net/news/coventry-named-most-dangerous-city-12408683

35. *Soccernomics* is a soccer book that studies different countries and takes into account such things as population, income per capita, and experience when figuring in the success or failure of club and national teams.

36. Simon Kuper and Stefan Szymanski, *Soccernomics* (New York: Nation Books, 2014), 388.

37. It's easier to turn confident dribblers into possession-oriented passers than it is to turn possession-oriented passers into confident dribblers.

38. "Brian Clough." *Soccertactics.com*, *The 21 Tactics Game*. Accessed April 25, 2017. http://www.soccertactics.com/top/brian-clough/.

39. "Brian Clough." *Soccertactics.com*, *The 21 Tactics Game*. Accessed April 25, 2017. http://www.soccertactics.com/top/brian-clough/.

40. "Brian Clough." *Soccertactics.com*, *The 21 Tactics Game*. Accessed April 25, 2017. http://www.soccertactics.com/top/brian-clough/.

41. WESTEND126. "Brian Clough interview after his retirement – 26th April 1997 – Football Focus." Filmed April 1997. YouTube video, 08:55. Posted March 3, 2015. https://www.youtube.com/watch?v=RkiNoF93cYw

42. Colonists were not allowed to go past the Appalachian Mountains.

43. *Fox Sports 1 (FS1)*. "Bundesliga Pregame." Fox Sports, August 26, 2016.